THE GODDESS IDUNN
IN
POETRY AND MYTH

MARIA KVILHAUG

TLS

ISBN13: 978-1-959350-14-9

Set in: Bright Sunday 20/33pt, Luminari 22pt, Georgia 15pt, Symbola 10pt

©The Three Little Sisters
USA/CANADA

-Image of the authors own sacred space for the goddess Iðunn-

30. Iðunnarkenningar.
Hvernig skal kenna Iðun-
ni? Svá, at kalla hana
konu Braga ok gætandi
eplanna, en eplin ellilyf
ásanna.[1]
Snótr.
Mey, Þas kunni Ellilýf
Ása.

Mæra Mey, Stærandi
Mun Hapta

Brunnákr Bekkjar Dís.

Ǫlgefn.[2]
Asa Leika.
Dís Forvítin.
Yggdrasils Frá.
Ivallds Ellri, Yngsta
Barni.
Álfa Ættar.
Nanna Syrgjandi.
Gjallar Sunnu Gátt.

Veigr Selja.
Iórunn.
Svanna.[3]

Hon er ok ránfengr Þjaza
jötuns, svá sem fyrr er
sagt, at hann tók hana
braut frá ásum. Eftir þeiri
sögu orti Þjóðólfr inn
hvinverski í Haustlǫng.

Ásu er svá rétt at ken-
na at kalla einn hvern
annars nafni ok kenna
við verk sín eða eign eða
ættir.[4]

30. Metaphors for Iðunn
(How shall Iðunn be referred
to? By calling her Wife of
Bragi, the Keeper of the
Apples, and the apple are the
Aesir's Age Cure.
Eloquent, Wise Woman.
The Maiden who Knows the
Age Cure of the Aesir.
The Precious Maiden who
increases the Joy of the
Gods.
The Goddess of the Benches
of the Water-Source-Field.
Ale-Provider.
The Lover of the Gods.
The Knowledge-Hungry
Goddess.
The Seed of Yggdrasill.
The Youngest Child of the
In-Ruler's Elders.
Elf-Kind.
Grieving Woman.
The Guardian of the Sun of
the Resounding River in Hel.
The Drink-Willow.
Steed-Woman.
Swan.
She is also Thiazi Jǫtunn's
booty in accordance with
the story told above about
his abducting her from the
Aesir. Thióðolf of Hvinir
composed a passage based
on that story in Haustlǫng:
[The poem is quoted]
It is also normal to refer to
the Aesir by calling one by
the name of another and
referring to him by his deeds
or possession or descent.

---

1 Skaldskaparmál 30
2 Haustlǫng
3 Hrafnagaldr Óðins
4 Skaldskaparmál 30

Contents

Iðunn Part 1: Skaldskaparmál

INTRODUCTION

This is the introduction to the first part out of three in a lecture trilogy or three part series where I will be going through everything there is to know about the goddess Iðunn in our sources. If you look up Iðunn in some textbook or online, you might find that she is described either as a goddess of youth or a goddess of love or fertility. I have been trying to find out why she is described this way, since I could not find anything in the sources that actually proved that she was either a goddess of youth or of fertility. The only reasoning I could find were these very simple words in Rudolf Simek's Dictionary of Northern Mythology. Now, this book is a treasure in so many ways, not the least because it gives you an overview over which sources one may look up to find something about a certain mythical character, and also because it gives you an overview of many of the different approaches and different understandings that are at large today, and also where there is consensus between scholars. But I have to say I was disappointed when I looked up Iðunn. The conclusion reads:

"If Iðunn was indeed venerated as a goddess in pagan times, she would belong to the fertility goddesses, because of her apples."

There you go. Because of her apples. It's that simple. Like with the Adam and Eve story - from the Bible, you know - that is all about fertility too, is it not? Because of the apples. I mean, that story involves apples, too. The Bible's story must needs be all about a fertility cult, and Adam and Eve must of course be fertility idols. Right?

Oh, I am going SO into that today.

Iðunn is the goddess who is most famous for being abducted, but who hides oh so many deeper aspects, once we dive into her myth.

Yes, I said myth, because, for all we know, there is only one myth in which Iðunn clearly plays a central role – the one where she is abducted and later rescued, as told in the 9th century Skaldic poem Haustlǫng and elaborated by Snorri Sturluson in the Skaldskaparmál.

I made a live lecture in Norway back in 2018 about this subject, before a crowd of actual Heathens at Idavollen during an event in which Iðunn was the focal point of that day's ritual. After speaking, I was invited to attend my first actual blót as practiced by some modern Heathens in Norway. I had of course mentioned the Edda poem Forspjallsljóð or Óðinn's Raven Galdr, but only because Iðunn is described with several poetical metaphors in stanza 6 - something I will get back to in this lecture series. The point here is that; During this ritual, that I was so fortunate as to be a part of, a re-enactment of this mysterious Edda poem, the Hrafnagaldr, was played out, showing Iðunn as the main female character of that poem, and showing that this mysterious Edda poem was another way of telling the same story - a story of the loss of the goddess.

That was quite the revelation to me, that there is indeed yet another literary source about the myth about Iðunn, where I thought we had to contend ourselves with two. So of course, I delved into it and will dedicate the third and last part of this lecture series to the Raven Galdr. When I began to work with this lecture, it soon became apparent that it would be grand. Too long for just one lecture. Too long for two lectures. I have had to split the whole thing in three, and this allows me to go deeper into each part without losing your interest on the way due to too much and too long.

There are three main written sources about the goddess. The oldest is the Haustlǫng, a skaldic poem composed in the form that we know it as early as the late 9th century, which means the late 800ds and takes us back to deep pagan Viking Age times. The poem is, like all Skaldic poems, crammed with metaphors, kenningar and heiti, all alluding to matters that the poet back in his day could assume that everybody knew. Sadly, we today do not have the same cultural references, and it is the absolute truth that the poem simply cannot be understood by moderns unless we gain access to that cultural reference. We find that reference in Snorri Sturluson's Prose Edda, where he explains the metaphors of Skaldic poetry by telling us the whole prose story background. Since this prose version is completely necessary to know well before delving into the older, skaldic source, I will begin with the Skaldskaparmál version of the story. We need to know this prose version first - in order to make sense of the poetic versions.

I decided to call the whole series: Iðunn in Poetry and Myth – Skaldskaparmál, Haustlǫng and Hrafnagaldr Oðins. The first part, this part, is Iðunn part 1: Skaldskaparmál. The second part will be Iðunn part 2: Haustlǫng, and the final chapter will be Iðunn part 3: Hrafnagaldr Óðins.

In the **first part**, I will be introducing you to these three main written sources, and talk about some archaeological sources that might shed some light on the goddess.

Then I will delve in deep into the most well-known version of the story; Skaldskaparmál, and I will be talking about Snorri's purpose when he wrote his works about Norse myths. I keep seeing Snorri getting dismissed in arrogant and ignorant ways, and I intend to make it more than clear what we owe to him, and how it is possible to see the worth – how we MUST see the worth – of what he did for us and what he made possible for us, even as we must apply discernment with his works - just as we must with any other source.

Source criticism is necessary, but does not mean the same as source dismissal. It just means that we cannot look at any historical source without studying the context in which it was created, or without comparing it to other sources in order to check if it could be authentic information about what we are searching for – such as a pagan religious tradition.

I will also discuss all the information we do get in the Skaldskaparmál, preparing us all for the next chapter, the one where I will discuss the Haustlǫng version.

In the **second part**, I will introduce you to the basics of skaldic poetical metaphors, and then go through the first 13 stanzas of the Haustlǫng in both Norse and English translation. Haustlǫng is a skaldic poem, so we will be delving deep into the world of poetical metaphors and what they might tell us about the Iðunn myth. I will end up discussing what the two sources together – the skaldic poem and the prose version - may tell us about pagan ritual practices such as seiðr and blót, and what the whole myth may really be about.

In the **third part**, I will introduce you to a mysterious Edda poem called the Hrafnagaldr Óðins, Óðins Raven Galdr, and go through the entire poem in its original, with translations and analysis, and discuss whether or not it makes sense to see this poem as another version of the Iðunn-myth.

Our Literary Sources

Haustlǫng

Just to sum up our sources about Iðunn. They are all literary sources, at least at first glance. The oldest source we have is the 9th century Skaldic poem Haustlǫng by the Norwegian skald Þjóðólfr enn hvinverski or Þjóðólfr ór Hvini, which means Thióðolf from Kvina, who was born around the year 855, and who died sometime around the year 930. Norway was not converted to Christianity until a hundred years after he died. Thióðolf, our oldest source to the Iðunn myth, lived during the actual Viking Age, and was a pagan poet whose cultural roots as a Viking Age pagan scald, ran back centuries, if not millennia.

As I will get back to, Skaldic poems represent our oldest literary sources, dating back to actual pagan times, and composed by actual, pagan skalds. Their poems were not written down until much later, but the thing about Skaldic poetry is that each poem was composed in a fixed manner, fixed with poetical metaphors and a use of grammar and single-letter rhymes that is archaic - and impossible to change over time – that is why we say they are fixed – they could not be changed over time. They are our most certain authentic examples of the orally transmitted literature of the Viking Age.

This is probably different from the Edda poems. Most of the Edda poems that we know, in the form we know them, the form in which they were written down, were likely composed sometime between 900 and 1100 – during the age of conversion. You could probably say they are fixed too, what with rhyming and other rules of poetry, but they are less complex than the Skaldic poem and may perhaps more easily have been susceptible to change before or while they were written down. As such, the Edda poems may have been slightly altered with time and with the slow change of culture from being pagan to becoming Christian, so to what degree they are direct or indirect sources to actual, pagan mythology has been the matter of much dispute, although most scholars now agree that they can definitely be used as sources to pagan mythology - if we only apply some discernment.

When it comes to the Skaldic poems, these were remembered and written down in the exact same form as when they were first composed: As such, these are our only actual windows into the poetical minds of real Heathen, Viking Age skalds – they take us directly back to the 9th century. What that poem proves to us about the goddess Iðunn is that the goddess and her myth as we know it today was well-established even back in the deep Viking Ages.

It is also a whole well of poetical metaphors which describe both Iðunn and the other gods, Loki and Óðinn in particular, as well as giants and other powers, all present in that poem in meaningful, informative and interesting ways. I will of course get back to that. This poem - and skaldic poetry as such - will be the focal point of the second part of this lecture trilogy.

Snorri Sturluson

The second source is centuries younger than Haustlǫng, written down by the marvelous and esteemed Snorri Sturluson, who took it upon himself to explain both Skaldic and Edda poetry to young people back in the 1220. This was 220 years after the Icelandic parliament decided, after a 50-50 vote pro and con, to take Christianity as the main state religion. As you can see, the conversion was a democratic process, and this age-old, pagan regard for democracy also meant that, since 50 % of the population was still pagan, paganism was not outlawed until a century later. This means that by the time the first Norse texts were written down with Latin letters onto leather books, real pagans with an unbroken tradition still lived, and still existed.

Perhaps they saw the worth of getting it all written down before it vanished, maybe that was why such incredible care was taken to preserve ancient poetry and lore. But now, a century after paganism had been outlawed, Snorri observed that young people in his day no longer understood the poetry of their ancestors. This poetry – Edda and skaldic poetry, was based on a system of metaphors that required a basic knowledge about the pagan worldview and pagan myths. Without such knowledge, you could not possibly understand what the metaphors meant. 220 years after the public conversion, Snorri observed that young people no longer understood these metaphors as easily as he had done or his predecessors, and so he took it upon himself to explain these metaphors for them – and for us who came after.

We all have Snorri to thank for the preservation of ancient poetry and for offering us a key to understanding them. We would have been nowhere if it was not for his work, when it comes to pagan mythology and pagan poetry. You see, by this feat, Snorri left to us a masterpiece of storytelling which is our singular main source for almost everything we today know about Norse mythology.

He wrote his work so that we could better understand that which has been subtly composed and hidden in symbols – how do I know that this was his exact intention with his work? Because he wrote so himself, right down in the Prose Edda. He directly says that his intention is to open up a means to understand that which has been hidden in symbols, that which had been cunningly and subtly spoken, that which had been conveyed to us in a language of riddles.

This masterpiece is now known as the Prose Edda. It is a teaching book about how to understand and decipher poetical metaphors. Incidentally, it explains myths we find in poetry, and records myths and also original poems that have otherwise been lost from us. He also wrote an explanation of the myth about Iðunn's abduction, basing himself on the much older, poetical work of his Heathen predecessor, Thióðolf. Snorri's medieval prose version of this myth explains the older and more archaic, poetical version.

Hrafnagaldr Óðins eða Forspjallsljóð

Iðunn is also mentioned in a mysterious poem known as Óðinn's Raven Charm – Hrafnagaldr Óðins, which has always been a very widely discussed poem. It is clearly an Edda poem, although there have been doubts about how old it is and whether it deserves a place in regular translations of Edda poetry. The poem has one stanza that is clearly about the goddess Iðunn falling down from her place in the universe – the world tree – and there is a good reason why some scholars have seen the whole poem as another version of the original Iðunn-myth; the loss of the goddess and what that means to the gods. I will go in-depth in this poem in the third part of this lecture trilogy. For now, let us discuss other sources that are not written sources.

NON-LITERARY SOURCES

When we are looking for ancient, pagan gods, goddesses and other powers, we must of course look to other sources which may clarify the position of that being in the actual, religious lives of human beings who lived back then.

We *must never presume* that a character's importance in written sources necessarily reflects its importance in the religious practices and beliefs of the people who actually lived. So we look for other traces in other sources: runic inscriptions, place-names and archaeological finds, especially in the form of artworks and symbolism.

Runic inscriptions **DO** sometimes invoke or describe characters that we know from mythology, providing yet another source to how these beings were worshiped or invoked. But as far as I know, there is no mention of Iðunn in any runic inscription. But that is also true about many other gods, and it is also true that the vast majority of runic inscriptions are more concerned with practical issues, or made in memory of some departed love one. So Iðunn's apparent absence does not mean she was not important.

Then we must look to *place-names*. Sometimes, place names show that gods who are not particularly important in the mythology that has been left down to us, may still have been extremely important in earlier ages or in certain regions. Scandinavia is littered with ancient place names that often show us where a certain god or goddess has been particularly worshipped, or where there are many gods worshipped together.

When we look to place-names, we find numerous well-known deities with their very own field, well, lake, grove, embankment, forest, mound, mountain, shrine or temple. These place names are usually put together by a word for "god" or "goddess", ether in plural or in singular, or by the actual name for a god or a goddess, set together with a word for shrine, temple, grove or natural locations. They may also use one of the god's many nicknames, one of their heiti.

Let me give you some examples:

☞I was born in Oslo, the capital of Norway. What the name ÅS-LO means is uncertain, but it is very old and may actually derive from the words ÅS and LO, meaning the Field of the Gods or Divine Field.[1]

I was born in a hospital called Ullevål, named after its location in the center of Oslo. The name is very old and literally means Ull's Embankment. There are other place-names involving the same god close by; there is a part of Oslo known as Ullern, which literally translates as Ull's Abode, and a place not far from Oslo called Ullensaker – Ull's Fields. In fact, the whole of south-eastern Norway is so crammed with place names referring to the god Ullr that we know for certain that he was once a very important god in this region – yet in the written sources, he is just mentioned a couple of times.

Snorri points out that Ullr is good at skiing and shooting with a bow, and in the Edda poem Grímnismál, the god Ullr is associated to Alfheimr and the god Freyr. But that is just about everything we know about this god, apart from him being of vital importance in certain regions – especially in south-eastern Norway, and we know this not from mythology, but from place names. What little mythology may have told us, even a tiny piece of the puzzle is better than nothing. It IS interesting that Ullr is indeed associated with Alfheimr – the World of the Elves. You see, Alfheimr - this was also how the entire region to the east of the Oslo fjord was also once known as Alfheimr – exactly within the region where we find the most place-names involving Ullr.

Not far from Ullevål in Oslo, we find another place called Torshov. This literally means Thor's Temple. So here, my friends, there was once a temple to the god Thor. Place names with Thor in them abound in Norway especially, where the place name material shows that Thor and Njǫrðr, for example, were more important than gods such as Óðinn. In Denmark and southern Sweden, however, Óðinn was clearly more important than he was in most parts of Norway, while Freyr was clearly more important in Sweden than in any other place. This goes to show that one of the earlier and more powerful dynasties of Sweden, the Ynglingar, regarded themselves as direct descendants of Freyr.

---

1 Gjerland, Leif (2008): «Navn i Oslo», Orio Forlag

We also find the names of otherwise unknown or little known goddesses who may have had a powerful significance in certain regions or in earlier ages, and the word "dis" for "goddess" both in plural and singular has been widely used for making place names everywhere. These valuable sources show us that the importance of gods and goddesses do not always reflect into the myths that we know about, and that their importance may have varied considerably from region to region, and also changed over time. However, when it comes to the goddess Iðunn, the place name material seems scant – I have not been able to find any place-names for Iðunn – at least not going by that name.

WHAT ABOUT ARCHAEOLOGY, ART?

Sometimes, we find images in ancient art that clearly illustrate a myth that we know about, and characters that we also know about from written sources. These archaeological finds are extremely valuable when it comes to show just how old roots they have, the myths that have been left down to us, and serve to prove that most of the myths we know about are indeed connected to hard fact finds dating back into the Viking Age and before.

But how do we know what gods and goddesses are on display?

If you take a look at the images below, we sort of know who is who or what it is about, based on what we know from stories about the gods, aspects and attributes. For example, the runic inscription with drawings show a scene that we know from the stories about a hero called **Sigurd Fafnisbani**, who appears in Edda poetry as well as in Vǫlsunga saga. The images come together with inscriptions that also tell us it is so. And so we know that the story was well known when this was carved into rock more than a thousand years ago.

A photograph of the Ramsund Carving which depicts the story of Sigurd Fafnisbani of discovered in Eskilstuna Municipality, Södermanland [Public Domain]

A carving of Gunnarr thrown into the Snake Pit. [Image from Public Domain]

Another image is from the Oseberg chariot, a tree-carving which shows a scene from a myth we find in the Edda poems as well as in the later Vǫlsunga saga; where the hero (or sort of anti-hero) **Gunnarr**, is thrown into the serpent pit by Atli the Hun, and a valkyria tries to rescue him, but comes to late, and Gunnarr is bit in the liver by a reptile who is really an animal hide for Atli's evil mother. And so we know that this story was already well-known in the form we know it by the year 834, which is from the very start of the Viking Age.

If we look at the **head of a man carved in wood**, we sort of "know" that it is Óðinn, mainly because of his missing eye, which is one of Óðinn's typical attributes – a symbol by which the god may be known. Next to the image of Óðinn, we see carved a man's face with his lips sewn together - and we recall the myth in which Loki has his mouth sewn together after losing a bet with a certain dwarf.

And the last image here is clearly of Óðinn arriving in the halls of Suttungr, wearing an eagle hide, receiving the drink of poetry from the giantess called Gunnlǫð – again, these are myths we know from the Edda poems.

Scan to view the carved head of a man thought to be Odin.

-Photo from the University Museum of Oslo, Photo Collection [CC BY-NC-ND 3.0

Odin in eagle form obtaining the mead of poetry from Gunnlod, with Suttung in the background (detail of the Stora Hammars III runestone, c. 700 CE) [Public Domain]

So we know that the Edda poems, which were written down some time AFTER the Viking Age, often refer to very old and very well-known myths from deep pagan times, what keeps getting confirmed by such archaeological finds. What these images may tell us, is that the myths that were written down during the 12th to 13th centuries were already well known during the pagan Viking Age, and that gods and heroes we have heard about, also had their places a long time before their stories were recorded on paper.

Or leather, whatever. However, it is hard to find an image from the Scandinavian Viking Age that, without doubt, is describing Iðunn. This is when we must take a cue from the archaeological finds that so perfectly illustrate known themes and characters from mythology, and from what Snorri says in his treatise about Edda and Skaldic poetry; that one character may show up in the guise of another, and that we may know them not by their name, but only by their attributes, their belongings, their relations, and their deeds. Let me read to you some passages from the Skaldskaparmál, ch.7, 30 & 28:

7:«The third speech-branch (category) is the one we call kenning, and this branch is constructed in this way; that we speak of Óðinn or Þórr or Týr or one of the Aesir or elves in such a way that with each of those that I mention, I add a term for the attribute of another god or make mention of one or other of his deeds; for instance, when we speak of Victory-Týr (Sígtýr) or Hanged Týr (Hangatýr) or Cargo-Týr (Farmatýr); these are Óðinsheiti (cover names for Óðinn), and we call these heiti, this is also the case with Chariot-Týr (Reiðartýr); this is a heiti for Thor.”

30: It is also normal to refer to a god by the name of another god, and know him by his deeds, possessions or relations.

28:«How shall we know Freyia? By calling her Daughter of Njǫrðr, Sister of Freyr, Wife of Óðr, Mother of Hnóss, Owner of the Fallen Dead (Eigandi Valfalls) or Owner of Sessrúmnir, Brisíngamen, she may be called Vanagoð (God of the Vanir), Vanadís (Goddess of the Vanir), The Weeping Beauty God, the Loving God. One may know all goddesses by naming another goddess, and know them by their works, deeds, or relations.

In Snorri's Prose Edda, Skaldskaparmál, we learn that a god or a goddess may indeed be known not by name only, but by attributes, properties, deeds and relations – and by nicknames describing their functions, and that they may easily borrow each other's names and heiti. All the gods and goddesses and any other power being - and even just things, people and animals, were also known by a whole list of heiti, a sort of nickname or cover-name that had a descriptive function.

You could replace the name of one god with another, and know the true identity by looking at attributes, functions, deeds and relations. The same is the case with a goddess or a giantess, you could call each by the name of another goddess or giantess, and add attributes, relations and deeds in order to recognize who you are really talking about.

As such, the identities of gods, goddesses and any other being in Norse mythology, are fleeting identities – their identity is not as fixed as we moderns are used to think. They frequently overlap with each other, and apply each other's names, and show up in each other's guises. In order to determine who we are really talking about, we must look to attributes, and functions, and relationships.

I once did a thesis called The Maiden with the Mead, about the theme of the mead-serving woman in the underworld. When it comes to function and attribute and what sort of context she shows up in, it is clearly the same character all the time. However, she appears as goddess, valkyria and giantess, even as a fylgja – always going by a different name.

Understanding this, my friends, is the key to understanding the hidden messages in Old Norse myths – to understand that one character and one event may be described in a thousand different ways and with a thousand different names. In the same way, we must look to attributes and functions when we look for gods and myths that we know in ancient art. And since the name is in fact not that important, since a deity could always be known by many different names, we may want to put the name Iðunn aside and rather look for what is TYPICAL of her. And since fruits, apples and nuts are important symbols associated to Iðunn, these are the attributes we must look for. This is when it gets interesting.

Matronae: The Mothers

When we put the name Iðunn aside and only look for the attributes that she is famous for, or in more academic terms; the iconography of this goddess, then we do in fact find evidence - a LOT of evidence! Just not where we thought we were supposed to look. There was indeed a goddess – or several goddesses - associated with apples, nuts and youth – and her iconography was central in the Iron Age religion of Northern Europe – and she has very old origins. That goddess is also part of a greater tradition which archaeology has shown to be a central theme of Iron Age, Germanic religions: the veneration of the so-called Mothers. Thousands of such altars dedicated to the mothers have been found all across northern European continent dating back to the late Roman Iron Age.

The altars have been made in Roman style and with Roman letters on them – but these Latin descriptions clearly show that most of the mothers were Germanic, while some may have been Celtic. The altars were indeed found in the regions where Germanic peoples lived, and some where Celts lived. These many altars to Iron Age goddesses are clearly fitting into the same category, insofar as they share iconography in every way possible. They are seated, enthroned, perhaps, like the oracles of old. They sit either alone or in groups of three, six or nine. They always carry a basket of fruits in their laps. By the rules of poetry and recognition I have told you about, this basket of apples is an attribute that serves to recognize the character behind.

The throne of the oracle is another important attribute, although we will have to wait until the third part of this lecture before we can discuss the evidence for Iðunn being another oracle goddess. It is only in the Raven Galdr that Iðunn is given the role of oracle. If they are seated alone in the shrine, they are given the Latin title of Dea – which means goddess, followed by a name that may actually have been a name, or else just a descriptive nickname, a heiti chosen in order to invoke a particular aspect of the goddess. If they come in groups, they are sometimes also referred to as deae – goddesses – but more commonly as Matronae – which means mothers. The title of Matronae is always followed by a descriptive name or nickname, again, the name is not the important thing, the important thing I what sort of power - what aspect of their powers – that you wish to invoke with this altar to the mothers.

To sum it up: The title of goddess, usually in the singular form, or mothers, usually in the plural form, come together with names that are clearly Germanic (or sometimes Celtic), even if the letters are in Latin. These altars were results of a time when many different cultures lived closely together for generations on end, for hundreds of years; Roman style art and the writing and reading of Roman letters became common, even as the mythology and religion behind that art remained the same native kind – and perhaps there was indeed a blooming of this native goddess-cult at this exact time.

This was an age of migration and war, many people losing their homes and moving away – perhaps the ancestral mothers and goddesses of the people served to tie them back to roots that they were slowly losing? One of the most common iconographies in these altars, carved in stone, is the seating of a young maiden in between the older women, seated there with a basket full of apples. Often, the elder women are also holding baskets of fruit. There may be other symbols present, but the basket of fruit is by far the most common.

An altar of the Aufanian Matronae, excavated in the Bonn Minster (Rheinisches Landesmuseum Bonn). Fiosher, H [CC BY-SA 4.0]

Relief of a seated Nehalennia between a dog and a basket of loaves [Photo from Mystic Mabel: CC BY-SA 2.0]

NEHALENNIA

The most important of all these mother or goddess characters is the goddess Nehalennia. Back in 1647, the Netherlands, sea levels sunk considerably and revealed a Roman Iron Age, 2nd century temple that had vanished in the sea more than a thousand years earlier.

In this temple to the goddess Nehalennia, she is nearly always depicted with a basket of fruit or nuts, either in her lap, by her left side, or both.

She may also appear together with a dog to her right, at the other side of where the fruit is. In Norse mythology, the dog – and the wolf – always symbolize the underworld, the guardians of the gates of Hel. These dogs or wolves are often associated with various ladies – giantesses - of the underworld, such as Hel, Hyndla, Hyrrokkin, and, interestingly, Skaði too. It is almost as if both Iðunn and Skaði, who appear in the same main myth, are BOTH represented in the image of Nehalennia – flanked by the dog on one side, and symbols of life and new seed on the other.

I have always felt that there is a connection between the two female characters of the myth, that Skaði is the other side of Iðunn, but it is only in the Raven galdr, that I will discuss in the third part of this lecture series, that Iðunn is in fact said to change shape and donning the wolf hide. We may remember that the face of Hel is half rotten as a dead woman, and half rosy like a lively young maiden. The life-giving maiden and the death-taking giantess keep appearing side by side in many myths, like Freyia with Hyndla, Sínmara with Menglǫð, Iðunn with Skaði.

Nehalennia's name has been interpreted in several different ways, the two most important of them either associating her to death, or else to abundance and provision. She is also associated with the conch, the ship, a throne in which she sits, exactly like we hear descriptions of oracles in ancient sources, including Germanic ones, and also a drinking horn, which was also a very important symbol of the Viking Age and Iron Age in Scandinavia. You may have heard of the Maiden with the Mead – a phenomenon I have covered before and will cover again. The mead-serving lady in the underworld may take the form of goddess, valkyria or giantess; yet her function and her attributes are the same.

FERTILITY GODDESS?

Whenever we find images of women carrying fruits or nuts in ancient times, we will quickly hear speak of a "goddess of vegetation" or a "goddess of fertility". If you google or check out typical source literature about Norse mythology, one will quickly discover that Iðunn is regarded as a "fertility goddess", simply explained with her association to apples, nuts and youth. As I said; I was truly disappointed when I looked up Iðunn in an otherwise highly esteemed work; the Dictionary of Northern Mythology by Rudolf Simek. Here, Simek concludes that "if Iðunn was really venerated in pagan times, it would be as a fertility goddess, because of her apples. Yeah, right, of course, how could apples ever symbolize anything but fertility, right?

Is this really that accurate?

If we look at these scenes, here, illustrating the Bible, we can see a lot of fruit, naked bodies, snakes, leaves and other symbols that would definitely have been dismissed as «fertility-symbolism» if it had been the iconography of pagan art. By the logic of Simek before, the apples alone are enough to categorize this myth as the myth of a fertility cult. But we know that it is not. The Biblical iconography of life in Eden before the "Fall" does not allude to a "fertility cult". We know this.

Based on the typical criteria for calling something a "fertility" god or a "fertility myth", another "fertility myth" can clearly be found in the Bible, featuring two "fertility idols" and a "phallic serpent god" in what must clearly have been a "fertility cult"

[Left: The Garden of Eden with the Fall of Man by Jan Brueghel the Elder and Pieter Paul Rubens, c. 1615, depicting both domestic and exotic wild animals such as tigers, parrots and ostriches co-existing in the garden. Public Domain 1615. Right: Original Sin, by Michiel Coxie. Public Domain. 1510-1550]

We know that the nakedness symbolizes innocence, and that fruit symbolizes forbidden knowledge, and that the snake symbolizes the adversary, the one who tempts humankind into breaking God's law; to not ever eat of the fruit of knowledge, lest we become as divine, immortal and wise as god himself. The knowledge that could make human beings reach the same level as God and achieve immortality by eating the fruit of knowledge. And this was the very source of sin and the end of paradise in the Biblical myth about fruits, snakes and naked human beings.

In other words; despite being sinful to eat, the apples, or fruits, of the bible myth symbolize divine knowledge and immortality. They have nothing to do with fertility at all. So we may ask ourselves why fruit in Biblical mythology symbolizes knowledge and immortality, while fruit in pagan mythologies automatically represents a fertility cult?

The answer is simple: It does not.

In Norse mythology, the **apples obviously represent the return of youth and life** from age and death, but the context is obvious; it is not about fertility, it is about what makes the gods into gods in the first place; the apples of the goddess represent the key to immortality, the key to eternal resurrection, the key to why the gods are gods and able to live forever. They mean exactly the same as what they meant in the Bible; divine knowledge and immortality.

The only difference is that paganism did NOT deem it sinful to seek such things. In fact, most pagan, pre-Christian myths that revolve around fruit, do show that the fruit - also in pagan mythologies - symbolizes exactly the same as fruit does in the Bible; divine knowledge and immortality. The Old Testament did not appear in a vacuum. It was recorded in a time and place where fruit symbolized divine wisdom and immortality, and continued to be so when Christianity appropriated this book. There are many such fruit-mythologies in the ancient world, such as the Hesperides in Greek mythology.

The Garden of Hesperides by Ricciardo Meacci. Public Domain [1856-1900]

The Hesperides were a group of nymphs who guarded the apples of immortality. There are many different Greek sources to these nymphs, and they appear either as one, three, four or seven women, daughters of the goddess of the Night, clear-voiced, and with many different names. In pagan religions, this form of divine knowledge is sacred. In Christianity, it is sinful to seek it. But that is about the only difference.

THE LIKES OF IÐUNN

As mentioned, in the Iron Age we find iconography or symbolism associated with Iðunn in Norse myths, among other things with the goddess Nehalennia in the Netherlands, who was associated with apples and other fruits, nuts, as well as the throne and staff of the oracle, dogs, shells and ships. She had many altars, and around the year 200, there was a huge temple in Netherlands containing more than 40 such altars in her honor. The temple was flooded and sank into the ocean like a Templar Atlantis. The temples and its many altars to the goddess reappeared in 1647. Incidentally, this was just a few years after the Poetic Edda manuscript – the only almost whole manuscript, also reappeared after centuries of being hidden away by some mysterious family in Iceland.

The meaning of her name is much debated, but could either derive from Latin necare, which means to kill, and which associates her to the diverse goddesses of death (or perhaps to the one goddess of many names, death personified)?. We see that she has a dog on one side, and in Norse myths, it is the ladies of the underworld who are associated with dogs and wolves, such as the famous Hel-Hound.

But her name may also have Germanic origins and have something to do with ships and harbors, and sets her in connection to the god Njǫrðr and perhaps with that mysterious sister it is said that he might have been married to, and who may be identical to the Iron Age Nerthus, a goddess associated with a lake and drowning. Which also gives associations to the Norse ocean giantess Rán, another goddess of the dead, specializing in the drowned.

Nehalennia is one of the Iron Age goddesses who are shown alone. But the symbols on her altars are very similar to the iconography that we find over the whole of Northern Europe during this era. Because the altars had Latin inscriptions, we know that they were dedicated to the so-called Matronae, the Mothers, who are often also referred to as Deae- goddesses, in the same contexts.

The term Mothers and Goddesses are used interchangeably, although "goddess" is the most common term when the altar is dedicated to a single goddess, while "mothers" is the most used term when the altar is dedicated to a collective of goddesses. When it comes to the iconography – that is, the shape and appearance, the symbolism, that is commonly applied to these little altars to Iron Age goddesses or mothers, they are almost identical to each other.

The most common feature is in fact the basket of apples, fruits or nuts in the laps of the goddesses – and the central positions of the youngest maidens in the group. So by normal standards, as I told you about before, it has been easy to just assume that they are part of a "fertility cult". However, it is our fortune that the Germanic and Celtic people who used this Roman style of making altars, also used Latin letters describing exactly who these ladies were. We are in fact given names – Germanic names, mostly, carved with Latin letters. And these names are descriptive.

If you listened to the introduction to this video, I listed a whole lot of descriptive names and metaphors for Iðunn, showing that she had many of the kind. The same is true for these Mothers; The inscriptions invoking the goddesses are like kenningar, like heiti, poetical metaphors and nicknames abounding, but really describing the same sort of power – a collective of goddesses who sometimes appear as one. And the names tell us a lot about them, and a lot about why it is pointless to narrow them down to the icons of a so-called "fertility cult".

I will tell you this in advance: even if we translate the Latin inscription as "mothers of this" or "goddess of that", these are not actual names, and neither are these powers particular for the function of these specific goddesses or mothers. Rather, these altars were either raised in order to just honor the divine ancestral mothers of a particular tribe, place, geographical location, natural formation or even a particular tribal federation or a military regiment.

Or they were raised in order to invoke particular and desired qualities and functions then and there, like in a prayer or an invocation. In some altars, the person who sponsored the altar, and his intentions and wishes are directly described and the man who sponsored it is even named.

I say "his" and "man", because, contrary to what is often also assumed, the mothers did not belong to the realm of women or to some separate cult of women – in absolutely every case where we learn the name and tribe of the person who let raise the altar, it is a man's name.

The mothers belonged to all the people, and men were evidently as devoted to these goddesses as women were. As we shall see, the inscriptions show that fertility is not the central issue.

Rather we are dealing with powers of magic, fate, fortune, protection and natural powers. I shall now read to you various titles of the mothers which appear in one or several altars found, dating back to the 2nd century AD.

While listening, I suggest you keep in mind all the different words that have been used to describe Iðunn in mythology.

※

Goddess of True Wealth
Mothers of Magic
Mothers of the Fate Wheel
Mothers of the Fenced Marchlands
Beer Mothers
Mothers of Both Sides of the Border

-In these titles lie the intention of having raised the altar: in order to address the goddesses in order to affect one's wealth, magical influence, or one's destiny, to get a good brew, or to honour some border treaty by raising an altar to the mothers of both sides of the border.

※

Mothers of Abundance
Goddess of Seafaring
Goddess of Hidden Death
The Mothers of the Anesus River
The Generous Kinswomen Mothers

-In these altars lie prayers for abundance, safe sea voyage, and an appeal to death — maybe as a curse on someone, or else as a way of placating Death.

One is also addressing the mothers of a particular river, for what reason I do not know, and the latter seem to refer to ancestral mothers who still had a finger in the play of life, and appealing to their generosity.

This reminds me of the concept of the ættarfylgja, the ancestral mother who continued to follow her descendants in the shape of a divine fylgja, affecting their fates.

※

Mothers of the Rivers
The Necklace-Carrying Goddess
Mothers of the Justice Court,
The Hard-Working, Providing Goddess
Mothers of the Amenau Rivers

-Here we see invocations or prayers or spells addressing the powers that rule the mighty rivers on which the people depended.

We see addressed a mysterious, necklace carrying goddess who must needs bring the later goddess Freya to mind.

The Bronze and Iron Ages have yielded several figurines of an important goddess associated with a necklace. We see that the goddesses may be invoked for justice during a law court, or for getting fruit out of hard work.

Ӱ

*Mothers of Birds, the High
Mothers,
Goddess of Rulers or Ruling
Goddess
Goddess of Oaths.
Goddess of Battle*

-I am pretty sure that altars
raised to the goddess of oaths
was a way of cementing an
important oath. And goddesses
have been associated with
birds since the Stone Age. The
Goddess of Rulers may have
been important to someone's
sovereignty, another ancient
theme invoking the sacred
marriage, where the king must
symbolically marry the goddess
of the fate of the land and
the people in order to claim
rulership. A goddess of battle
and mothers of birds, well, they
sort of speak for themselves.

Ӱ

*Goddess of Battle and Goals.
Goddess of Masculinity.*

-Yes indeed. They had a
goddess for THAT too!

Ӱ

*Goddess of Works.
Goddess of Birch Trees.*

-Now that is specific. But the
birch may have symbolized
something other than a
particular tree. In Norwegian
folklore, birch branches were
used to ritually cleanse the
house of spirits after a time of
intense ritual such as Yule.

Ӱ

Goddess of Hot Springs.

-But yes of course. They
bring healing to sore bodies.
And naturally, we do have
The Oracle Goddess. In Norse
myths, goddesses such as
Frigg, Freyia and Gefion are all
said to be oracles in some way
or another.

Ӱ

*Water Mothers. Goddess of
Martial, as in War-like Honor.
Mothers of the Owl Groves*

– what do Owl groves
symbolize, but seeing clearly
were others only see into dark
nothingness?
Or perhaps these were
particular groves, pagan
temples, associated with
goddesses who took the form of
owls? Perhaps.

Ӱ

*Mothers of the River Streams.
Mothers of the Otter Dams.*

-Of course we must have
goddesses for otter dams.

Ӱ

Mothers of the Thurse's Power

– the Thurs has a rune of its
own – this is an invocation of
the giant powers, of magic,
dark magic, perhaps.

𐌖

The Desired Goddess.

-Brings goddess Frigg
to mind; the Beloved. And
more specifically:

*Mothers of the Southern
Tribes.*

-The goddesses associated
with a particular tribal
federation to the south
of whatever these people
thought was the central
point. Making altars in their
honor could have been a way
of honoring the agreement
between the tribes who went
into federations.

𐌖

*Mothers of the Original Rulers
Goddess of Swift Healing –*

-This altar was raised in
order to get, you know, swift
healing from something.

𐌖

The Mothers who Follow –

-Here we have something we
recognize from later sources,
the concept of followers,
fylgjur, goddess spirit beings
who follow a human being
through life, affecting our fates.

𐌖

Mothers of Success.

-Right, let us pray to the
Mothers of Success whenever
we need success"

𐌖

*The Clairvoyant, Magical
Water-Mothers.*

-Someone wanted to know
something about their fate
here, I am pretty sure.

𐌖

*The Loyal Mothers
The Honored Mothers
The Old River Mothers
The All-Providing
Mothers
The Great, Life Giving
Mothers
The Powerful, Creative
Mothers*
Here is a favorite of mine.

The inscription reads
DEAE GAMALEDAE.

-This is to show that even
when in Latin, we may
recognize the Germanic
words that make up the title.
Gamaledae is clearly the
same as Norse Gamal Edda

– Old Great Grandmother.

-They actually had an Old
Great Grandmother Goddess.
Then we have The Generous,
Providing Mothers

*The Old Rivers' Mothers
Mothers of the Borders -*

-Between tribes, I assume,
or between nations – here,
the goddesses are invoked to
protect the borders.

*Great, Generous, Providing
Goddess –*

-Well, this providing thing
keeps repeating itself. In
Old Norse myths, we have a
goddess called Gefiun, which
means "the Provider". The
short form is Gefn, which
means the same but is said to
be one of Freyia's many cover
names – a Freyiuheiti.

And we also have the
Mothers of Geeze.

-This may seem absurd, but
**waterbirds do have a place
of their own in northern
cosmologies, often
representing goddesses,
valkyriur or the souls of
people.**

*The Old Rivers Mothers
Mothers of the Eastern
Border
The Providing Goddess –
again –*

*Mothers of Oaks, Mothers of
Mountains, Mothers of Grain
Goddess of Sacred
Abundance
Mothers of Divine Support
Mothers of Destiny
The Clothing Mothers
Mothers of House
Constructions*

So here in the end, I gathered
some of the many Mothers
dedicated to particular tribes,
military regiments or tribal
federations or even just
location (tribes of the south,
tribes of the east).

This goes t show that some
sort of ancestral mother
worship may be a part of the
general worship of mother-
goddess collectives:

*Mothers of the Rumanehae
and the Avitinehae Tribes
Mothers of the Condrusi
Tribe.*

*Mothers of the Frisian
Ancestors
Mothers of the Germans
Mothers of the Ancestors of
the Cannanefatium Regiment
Mothers of the Roman
Settlement – that would be
Germans living within the
borders of the Roman Empire.
Mothers of the Gods of the
Southern People
Mothers of the Eastern tribes*

"FERTILITY IDOL" – A MODERN CONCEPT

The idea that these ladies have to do with a fertility cult becomes pretty lame when you see all the different functions that come to light in view of these Iron Age altars to goddesses - who do not appear to be very different from one another when it comes to attributes or iconography. These are not names, these are descriptions, much like all the Iðunnarkenningar I read up to you at the start of this video.

These descriptions seem to be describing various aspects of a group of female deities - or singling out one representative. They cover a very wide array of functions – they protect armies, borders, rivers, tribes, offer provisions, healing, magic, divination, success, safe journeys, martial honor and masculine virtue and so on – and they are all represented as
   • Seated on thrones like oracles,
   • carrying a basket of fruits in their laps, as such, associating all of them with Iðunn in Norse myths. And as we shall see in the Iðunn-myth; Fertility is evidently not the only - not even the main - ingredient here.

In fact, the term "fertility" and "fertility goddess" are in themselves modern terms. Terms that make it easier for US to put mythical characters into boxes and categories, while they say absolutely nothing meaningful about these gods. In the actual sources we have, there is no single god or goddess who is referred to as "goddess of love", "god of war" or any other thing.

What realms they rule are far more fleeting and overlapping with others than such terms allow for, and far more diverse and many-faceted. Calling them "God of this or that" are modern ways of categorizing pagan gods in a way that did not exist in pagan times, when it was the other way around; one god or goddess could be named by countless different words describing their functions in particular contexts.

If we look closely on pagan myths where apples and fruits play a role, we shall quickly see that they have less to do with fertility and more to do with knowledge, sacred wisdom and immortality – just like in the Bible. Only that seeking such apples was considered holy, not sinful. So what I want you to do now, is to put away all ideas you might have about how to categorize Iðunn as a "Goddess of Youth" or "Goddess of Fertility" or "Goddess of Spring" or whatever other assumption you may have nurtured, please put all that away and listen to the actual stories and the actual words used, and let these stories and these words speak for themselves for a while.

SNORRA EDDA

Let us return to the written sources we have about Iðunn. Let us start with the youngest source, Snorri's Edda - the Prose Edda which dates back to the 1220s. As I told you to start with, the book was really a teaching book for young people who wanted to understand the metaphorical and allusive and allegorical poetry of their great grandparents. Incidentally, it has allowed us to figure out ways to understand Old Norse Edda and skaldic poetry, as well as provided us with a well of hints as to how to decipher the riddles, and even full A-B explanations of said poetry.

The Book is divided into two main parts; the Gylfaginning and the Skaldskaparmál. The first, Gylfaginning, which means; "The Illusions of the Sorcerer", refers mostly to Edda poetry, and explains Edda poems. It also introduces us to each god and goddess that Snorri deemed central.

In Gylfaginning, chapter 26, we may read:

«One is called Bragi. He is famous for being wise, and especially for eloquence and the art of rhetoric. He is the one who knows the most about skaldskáp, and after him, skaldskáp is also called «brag», and from his name comes the expression: «a brag of a man» or «a brag of a woman» about a man or a woman who knows how to use words better than others.

His wife is Iðunn. She hides, in her casket, some apples that the Aesir shall eat when they grow old, and then they become young again, all of them, and this is how it shall be until Ragnarok». Gangleri said; «I think these are great things, that the gods keep in Iðunn's care, and leave over to her loyalty»

Then said The High One, and laughed at the same time: «Once it nearly went wrong, and I can certainly tell you about it...»

This here says very little about Iðunn, other than that she has an important task as guardian of the apples of youth, and that she is married to a god famous for eloquence, poetry and wisdom. This marriage is, however, important. It means that Iðunn is a match to these qualities: Eloquence, poetry and wisdom. She is a goddess associated to art, learning and the weaving of words into good stories.

Images from the From the 18th century Icelandic manuscript SÁM 66 in the care of the Árni Magnússon Institute in Iceland.

What you see in these images are illustrations from a very old, medieval rendering of Snorri's Prose Edda, illustrations exactly from the myth of Iðunn, even if Iðunn is not present in any of the images. As said: In the first part of the Prose Edda, Snorri concentrated on the Edda poems. This part has been known as the Gylfaginning, the Visions of the Sorcerer. In the second part, Snorri moves on to explain skaldic poetry. This is called the Skaldskaparmál. Skaldskaparmál means "The Speech about the Art of Poetry", and it explains poetical categories and metaphors.

This textbook, this teaching book, this veritable thesis on Old Norse poetry by one of its last keepers, Snorri Sturluson, has a narrative setting and is a piece of poetry in itself. Snorri was a fantastic storyteller! One of the best, if you ask me. The narrative begins with the ocean giant Aegir coming to visit the Aesir in their hall. The gods prepare a great banquet in his honor, and the god Bragi, Iðunn's own husband, begins his speech about the art of poetry.

We are in chapter 1-4 of the second part of the Prose Edda, the Skaldskaparmál, my translation of which is below:

IÐUNN IN THE SKALDSKAPARMÁL

Ægir sækir heim æsi.
Aegir Invites the Aesir Home
[Skaldskaparmál 1, Prose Edda]

1: A man has been called Aegir [Terrifying One][2] or Hlér [Wind-(=Death)-Shielded][3]. He lives on that island which is now called Hlésey [Wind (Death)-Shielded Island].[4]

He was very knowledgeable/versed in magic [fjǫlkunnig]. He made a journey to Ásgarðr, and the Aesir could foresee his journey, and he was well received even though many of the things they did to entertain him were mere illusions.[5]

And when evening came and they were to drink, then Óðinn let carry into the hall swords that were so bright that they shone, and other light than this they had not while they were seated at the drinking banquet.
The Aesir came to the banquet, and the twelve who were to sit as judges sat down in their high seats, and they were the following gods: Thor, Njǫrðr, Freyr, Týr, Heimdallr, Bragi, Víðarr, Váli, Ullr, Hænir, Forseti, Loki.
The goddesses came to their seats just like the gods: Frigg, Freyja, Gefion, Iðunn, Gerðr, Sígyn, Fulla, Nanna.
Aegir thought it was all very splendid-looking. All the walls were decorated with beautifully adorned shields. There was a lot of strong mead there, and a lot was drunk.

---

2 Otherwise associated with the ocean, a husband to the sea goddess Rán and their nine daughters.

3 Hlér – Wind-shield. Wind is a metaphor for death in Norse poetry, wind-shield for immortality, hence his name really means "The Immortal One".

4 Hlésey – the Island of immortality

5 Sjónhverfingum: Sight-Warpings: illusions

Next to Aegir sat Bragi. The two of them drank together and spoke, and Bragi told Aegir about many things that had happened to the Aesir, and he started thus:
Þjazi jötunn rænti Iðunni

Image from the From the 18th century Icelandic manuscript SÁM 66 in the care of the Árni Magnús-son Institute in Iceland.

WHEN SLAVE-BINDER THE DEVOURER STOLE IÐUNN
[Skaldskaparmál 2, Prose Edda]

2: Bragi said: «This here is the story about how three Aesir left home; Óðinn, Loki and Hænir[6] , and they traveled across mountains and wilderness, and there was very little to eat. And as they came into a certain valley, they saw a huge flock of oxen, and they took one ox and put it to the earth-oven [seyði]. And so they thought that they would soon eat and that the meat must have cooked, but when they opened up the earth-oven they saw that the meat was as raw as before. After a while more, they checked again. But the meat was not cooked now either, and they asked themselves how this could be possible.

Then they heard speech from the oak above them, and they agreed that the one seated up there was guilty of obstructing the cooking.

They looked up, and there sat an eagle, and he was not tiny.[7]

Then the eagle spoke: "If you will give me a good piece of your meat, then it shall soon be cooked."

---

6 In the Edda poem Vǫluspá and in Gylfaginning, Hænir ["Chicken"] is the god who offers the gift of thought/mind to the first human beings, alongside Óðinn's gift of inspiration. He represents "thought".

7 Ok eigi lítill – a typical Norse understatement. "He is not tiny" actually means that he is enormous, formidable.

They agree to that. Then the eagle descended from the tree, sat down on the fireplace and swiftly gathered both the legs and the torso.

Then Loki was angry, grabbed a huge wand, lifted it with all his might and struck it against the eagle's body. The eagle bolted and flew upwards, and the wand stayed as glued onto his back, and Loki's hands were as glued to the wand.

The eagle did not fly higher than that Loki's feet were still touching on rocks and rock piles and the roots of fallen trees, and he felt as if his arms were being pulled off his shoulders.

Images from the From the 18th century Icelandic manuscript SÁM 66 in the care of the Árni Magnússon Institute in Iceland.

He cried and begged the eagle to let him go free.

And the eagle said that he would never go free unless he swore that he should lure Iðunn with her apples out of Ásgarðr, and Loki promised this.

He was let free and went to his traveling companions. And nothing more is told about this journey until they returned home.

At the agreed time, Loki lured Iðunn out of Ásgarðr into a certain forest and said that he had found some apples there that he thought she would think particularly valuable and asked her to bring her own apples in order to compare them with the others.

Then came the giant/devourer Slave-Binder[8] in eagle's hide[9], and he took Iðunn and flew away with her to his homestead in Þrymheimr [The World of Drumming].[10]"

8 Slave-Binder the Giant: Þjazi jötunn (From Þiaza= to bind, capture, take as a slave). The fact that he is a giant in eagle's hide seated in the top of a huge tree is an allusion to an eagle mentioned in Gylfaginning 16, a "much knowing" (margs vitandi) eagle who sits in the top of Yggdrasill, the world tree. In the Edda poem Vafþruðnismál, the eagle is identified as another giant in eagle's hide, Hræsvelgr [Corpse Swallower], who by flapping his wings at the end of the universe (top of the tree) is creating all the winds of the universe, and these winds are alluding to mortality.

9 In eagle's hide = í arnarham

10 The World of the Drummer = Þrymheimr – from thruma- «to drum», make repetitive sound.

Loki náði Iðunni ok dráp Þjaza.
Lóki Saves Iðunn and Kills the Slave Binder
[Skaldskaparmál 3, Prose Edda]

3: "The Aesir went sick when Iðunn was gone, and they were soon getting grey and old[11].

Then they held Parliament and asked each other whatever each of them knew about the disappearance of Iðunn, and it was soon discovered that she was last seen when she left Ásgarðr in Loki's company.

 Then Loki was seized and led out to stand before the Parliament, there they threatened to torture and kill him. He was frightened then, and said that he would search for Iðunn in the Giant Worlds[12], if only Freyia would lend him the falcon hide that she owned.

And when he got the falcon hide[13], he flew north into the Giant Worlds and came one day to the devourer, Slave Binder. He had rowed out to the sea, and Iðunn was at home. Loki transformed her into the shape of a nut and held her in his claws as he flew the fastest he could. And when Slave Binder returned home and discovered that Iðunn was missing, he took his eagle hide and flew after Loki, and his wings were eagle-blown [wind in his wings].[14]

---

11 Iðunn was the goddess of rejuvenation and immortality – it is because of her that the Aesir enjoy divine immortality in the sense that their youth and life is regenerated when receiving the fruits of the goddess.

12 In the giant worlds = í Jötunheima

13 Falcon hide = Valshamr. The type of bird hide is a significant reference. In poetry, hawks and falcons are identifiable, the use of the word val for falcon is in itself a metaphor and gives association to the chosen dead, those who will achieve immortality. According to Snorri's Gylfaginning 16, a falcon/hawk called "Wind-Diminisher" (Vedrfölnir)sits between the eyes a large giant in eagle hide whose wings create all the unseen winds of the worlds of the universe. According to the Edda poem Vafþrúðnismál, this giant eagle's name is Hræsvelgr, «Corpse Swallower»(see The Poetic Edda – Six Cosmology Poems). As such, the giant in eagle's disguise, who sits in a large tree just like Slave Binder, represents mortality, his wings blowing the winds of death, while the "wind-diminishing" hawk/falcon, owned by Freyia but now worn by Loki, represents a hope for immortality.

14 tekr hann arnarharminn ok flýgr eftir Loka, ok dró arnsúg í flugnum: arnsúg = «eagle-blown». This is, again, a reference to the winds of mortality created by the giant in eagle hide, Hræsvelgr («Corpse Swallower»). As Loki is here rescuing

And when the Aesir saw that the falcon came flying with a nut in his claws, and the eagle after, they went out beneath the wall that encircles Ásgarðr, carrying huge piles of wooden splinters[15].

The falcon flew in above the wall and let himself fall down by the rock wall. Then the Aesir set fire to the splinters. The eagle could not manage to halt his speed when the falcon escaped him, and then the fire reached his feathers so that he could no longer fly.

The Aesir were now close, and killed Slave Binder the Devourer inside of the Divine Gate [Ásgrindr]; that slaughter is widely famous.

But Skaði [Injury], the daughter of Slave Binder the giant, took helmet and byrnie and all sorts of army-weapons and went to Ásgarðr to avenge her father. And the Aesir invited her to sit and offered her compensation and truce, and the first thing she should have for compensation was to choose for herself a husband among the Aesir. But she could only choose him by the feet, more she could not see.

Then she saw a pair of man-feet that were unusually beautiful, and she said; "I choose this one. Few things are ugly on Balder." But it was Njǫrðr from Ship's Harbor[16]. In her truce terms, she had also demanded that the Aesir should manage something she was certain they would never be able to; and that was to make her laugh.

Then Loki had an idea. He tied a rope to the beard of a goat, and the other end to his own genitalia. And they took turn pulling and yielding, and both of them were screaming loudly. Finally Loki rolled over and fell right into the lap of Injury [Skaði], and then she laughed. Then there was agreement between her and the Aesir."

---

the goddess of immortality from a giant in eagle hide, and there is an additional reference to the blowing of eagle-winds in his wings as he tries to get away with the goddess of regeneration, the entire story is about immortality versus mortality.

15 Wooden splinters = lokarspánir

16 Njǫrðr ór Nóatúnum – the Vanir god of winds and waves.

Af Ætt Þjaza.
Of the Slave-Binder's Lineage
[Skaldskaparmál 4, Prose Edda]

4:"It is also said that Óðinn offered to her the added compensation of taking Slave Binder's eyes and hurled them up to heaven, and made two stars out of them."

Then said Aegir: "Great it seems to me that the Slave Binder must have been. Do you know more of his lineage?"

Bragi said: "Ale Ruler[17] was his father named, and about him I can tell you something that you might think worthy of mention: He was particularly rich in gold. When he died, and the sons were to shift the inheritance among them, then they used that for a measure cup; if each should get his equal share of the gold, then each of them should swallow an equal number of mouthfuls of it. Slave-Binder was the first among the brothers, the second was Returns to Source[18], the third was Wanderer.[19]

And now we apply this saying amongst ourselves, that we call gold "the Mouth-Speech" of these giants. And in runes or poetry we hide the word "gold" in that way that we call it the "language" or the "words" or the "speech" of these giants."

Aegir said: "I think that is cunningly hidden in symbols [runes]. "[20]

---

17 Ölvaldi: Ale-Ruler – a reference to the precious mead, or Allvaldi = All-Ruler

18 Iði – the same root word that makes up the name Iðunn – "Stream Returning to Source"

19 Wanderer= Gangr. The giant trinity is a poetical/mythical formula that repeats itself numerous times in Norse myth, just as it does among the gods, essential to creation. The same characters and trinities may also take different names, riddles for the readers to be solved.

20 Þá mælti Ægir: "Þat þykkir mér vel fólgit í rúnum."

Design on purse lid from Sutton Hoo, Suffolk, 7th century AD – hawk chased by an eagle?

IMPORTANT ELEMENTS

I want you to briefly consider some of the important elements in this story, since we will return to the subject later, when we analyze the myth in view of this prose version compared with the older, poetic version. First of all, the story begins with a theme that repeats itself in Norse mythology, the theme of Three Gods traveling the world - in the beginning of time. This is significant. The other stories in which three gods travel the world at the beginning of time all lead to something essential.

- We have Óðinn, Víli and Vé, who, at the dawn of time, divide the body of the giant Ymir into countless parts that make up the physical universe. I have long since proposed that the meaning of Ymir's name is important here. I think that his name comes from Old Norse ýmr, which means a sound of a murmuring voice. Dividing this ur-sound into many parts is like dividing original sound into an orchestra of diverse tunes. This theme repeats itself in Norse mythology and has counterparts in other mythologies, such as the Old Indian notion that the whole world came out of Brahman's mouth in the form of a voice or a sound; Aoom.
- We have Óðinn, Hlóðurr and Hænir, who, at the dawn of time, walk on earth for the first time and find two pieces of driftwood, Ask and Embla. They offer to the two, to man and woman both, the gifts of breath and spirit, thought and mind, life-force and many beautiful colors.
- We have Óðinn, Loki and Hænir entering the world of the giants together, finding the Red Gold which symbolizes divine wisdom and which is a great theme in many other mythical and legendary stories – among the Red Gold is the ring Draupnir, which drips eight new rings like itself every ninth night. The ring goes down to Hel with Baldr, but is brought back from Hel by a hero who dares to travel into the underworld while still alive.

And then there is this, three gods walking the earth, Óðinn, Loki and Hænir, and it should now go without saying that the theme itself indicates that this is a myth of the origin of something very important. What is it, then? I think it is interesting that the equipment used to cook the ox is an Earth Oven.

In the medieval imagery we have seen, there is a great cauldron, but the poem Haustlǫng, and Snorri too, clearly state that we have to do with an Earth Oven, which means that it was dug inside the earth and cooked inside the earth. This in itself may be significant; This is something that happens within an earthly sphere, perhaps, or may have something to do with the Earth goddess herself, perhaps.

The word for Earth Oven that is used is a seyði. This does not mean that we are necessarily speaking of seiðr, as in a Norse tradition of magic, shamanism, witchcraft and oracular Divination. It does not automatically mean that, because even as the words sound similar, they have different etymology – there is nothing which clearly states that the seyði derives from the same word as seiðr – but it is extremely interesting to note that the poet has chosen this particular word- that sounds a lot like it. That poets played with sounds and similarities in order to reveal subtle meanings is a fact. The cooking of the ox in the seyði also leads to a journey into another world, a shamanistic aspect, which I do not think is coincidental.

Then we learn about a jǫtunn - a giant – in eagle hide, and he sits in the tree above, and he WAS NOT SMALL. This is typical Norse understatement humor and means that he was excessively, incredibly large. His name is Thiazi, which may perhaps derive from a verb, þiaza, which means to capture or bind (in slavery). As I have mentioned, we may know a character from its attributes and functions, so let us look at the attributes; a giant in eagle hide, sitting atop a tree, being incredibly huge.

We DO find other such characters in Norse myths.

In the Gylfaginning, Snorri mentions an eagle who sits at the very end of the universe, in the northern end, at the top of the ash Yggdrasill, which is a poetical metaphor for the universe. The giant in eagle hide creates all the winds that blow through the universe.

An Edda poem, Vafþrúðnismál, lets us know that the giant in eagle disguise who sits at the edge of the universe is called Hræsvelgr; that means Corpse Swallower, and he creates all the subtle winds that may not be seen by the human eye, but which permeate all the worlds and the entirety of existence; these are the winds of the force of mortality, death itself.

In Norse poetry, wind, breeze and weather is constantly used as a metaphor for death and mortality, like when Óðinn hung in the wind-swept tree. Places with names that means shielded from winds, wind-shielded or breeze-less, are places of immortality, such as the island where Aegir lives, or the grove where Freyr may finally meet his beloved, the breezeless grove of Barri.

SEIÐR

Since I suggested that seiðr may be a part of the theme of the story, I might point out that there is a staff involved, the staff that Loki uses to hit Thiazi between the shoulders, a staff which then glues itself to Thiazi in one end and Loki in the other. A staff, my friends, may very well allude to seiðr, and Loki himself is evidently something of a seiðr-performer.

Another possible hint towards a shamanistic variant of seiðr is the fact that Thiazi's abode is in Þrýmheimr. Þrýmheimr is also known as the realm of Þrýmr (Thrym) the jǫtunn who stole Thor's Hammer. Þrýmheimr is also the abode of Skaði, Thiazi's daughter, a realm of wolves and snow and mountains. And the name Thrym derives from the verb Þrúma – «to drum» (or make a rhythmic beat of any kind). As you may know, drumming or at least steady beat vibrations are often crucial to shamanistic séances that involve out of body travel into other worlds. And this story certainly involves journeys into other worlds.

FREYIA'S VÁLSHAMR

Then there is Freyia's válshamr. A vál is a heiti for falcon or hawk, so we do know that we are speaking of a Falcon or Hawk Hide – the one that Freyia owns but frequently lends out to Loki. We know several stories where this happens. However, vál is also a word for the chosen dead who come to Freyia or to Óðinn. As I see it, the válshamr is not just a bird hide, it is the Hide of someone who has been chosen to die and go to Valhalla or Freyia, which involves a form of immortality in the form of eternal resurrection and renewal. I already mentioned the eagle who sits in the top of the world tre, the eagle Hræsvelgr – "Corpse Swallower". Snorri lets us know that right between the two eyes of the eagle of death, the wind-source of the universe, sits a falcon.

The falcon is called Veðrfǫlnir: which means «Wind-Diminisher». The falcon is like a third eye of the eagle itself, and it is what can diminish the power of the eagle's winds, diminish the power of death itself. And rightly enough, when The Eagle of Death burns, Loki and Iðunn survive in the divine realm of the gods – they have re-achieved immortality and conquered death.

Freyja's Feather Cloak Published in Gjellerup, Karl (1895). Den ældre Eddas Gudesange. [Public Domain USA]

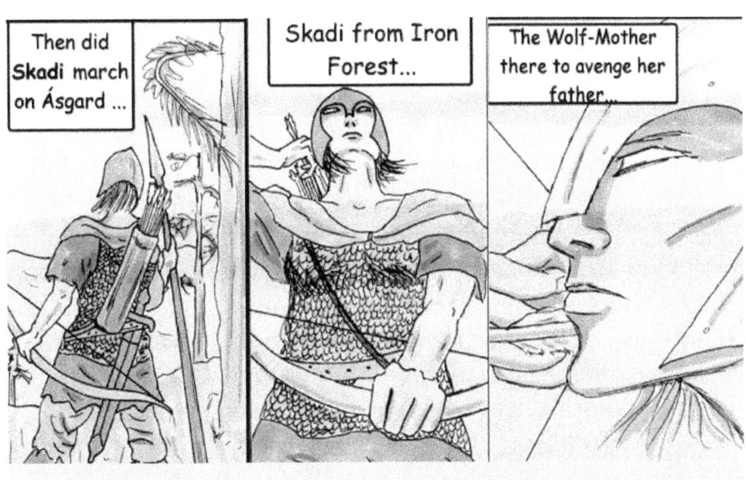

Drawn by Maria Kvilhaug

SKAÐI

In Snorri's version of this story, Skaði plays an important role, but only as the second chapter in a two-chapter story: She appears after everything has been solved with Iðunn and Loki. She is the consequence of all that has happened; the one who seeks justice and atonement for the wrongs committed, which from her point of view is the killing of her father. The giantess obviously has great power, for the gods do everything they can to appease her, making her father's eyes into stars in the heavens, offering her a husband of her own choice among the gods, and doing their best to make her laugh, even at the cost of a fellow god's dignity. Skaði also seems to represent the very opposite of Iðunn – dark, dangerous, deadly, her very name simply means "injury", or "harm".

She is a giantess, a hunter, a skiing goddess, perhaps the inventor of skis, she likes the mountains and the howling of wolves around her. In some skaldic poems, she has been identified as the mother of Sæmingr, who was the ancestral king of the Háleygja royal dynasty of northern Norway. The father was Óðinn, and Skaði was indeed said to have slept with the following three gods; Njǫrðr, Óðinn, and Loki. Only by Óðinn did she have children – several children, it is said, and a son who became a human king, or an ancestor to human kings in the northern parts of Norway. Skaði is, thus, not only a giantess with the status of goddess, but an ancestral mother to Viking Age dynasties.

In the Skaldic poem Haustlǫng, the story about Skaði is not mentioned. As soon as Thiazi is killed and Iðunn is rescued, Thióðolf turned to the other image on the shield that he was describing with poetry, and told the story about Thor's and Loki's journey to the halls of Geirrǫðr. But even Thióðolf indirectly refers to Skaði by three different kenningar in this poem: She is called Mǫrn, which means the Giantess, she is called Ǫndurdís, the goddess of skiing, which we know from other sources, and she is referred to as Bjarga-Gefn, the Providing Woman of the Mountains. The term Gefn for provider is frequently used for both goddesses and giantesses. It means "female Provider" and is also one of Freyia's heiti and the name of another goddess, Gefion, who is probably as identical to Freyia as her name is linguistically identical to the Freyiuheiti Gefn. However, since we are going to focus on the story as told in the Haustlǫng, we shall leave Skaði for now.

Epilogue to part 1:

We have reached the end of the first part of this lecture series. Some of you may be a bit surprised at how passive the goddess Iðunn is in this story. She is hardly even there, except that we know that she is there, we feel her, and it is more than clear just how important she is. She makes the difference between immortal god and mortal human, life and death for the gods. And yet, we do not hear that much from her. Why? Maybe it has something to do with what Iðunn really represents – something subtle, something that cannot be heard nor seen, yet which we know is there, and which we know is crucial to all existence, and to the lives of the gods.

Iðunn Part 2: Haustlǫng – A Skaldic Poem of the Viking Age

INTRODUCTION TO PART 2:

So, my friends, we have come to the second part of this lecture trilogy. Last time, I introduced you to the prose version of the story, the one told by Snorri Sturluson back in 1220-25. In order to sum it up:

We have a myth that starts with three gods wandering the Earth while the Earth was still young. As I told you before, three gods at the dawn of time constitute a theme that always means the start of something.

1. Óðinn, Víli and Vé emerged into the chaos of the universe and made it into an orderly, physical universe where beings could emerge and live.

2. Three giant maidens arrive and demand the creation of dwarves

3. As it says in the Vǫluspá, Óðinn, Hænir and Hlóðurr used the shapes of dwarves to walk the earth, and found two pieces of driftwood, Ask and Embla, the first man and woman. To them, Óðinn gave breath and spirit. Hænir gave mind and thought, and poetry itself. Hlóðurr gave them the life spark and many beautiful colors.

4. Three norns appear and decide the laws and fates of all living beings.

5. Óðinn, Hænir and Loki wander the worlds and discover the so-called Red Gold, a mysterious poetical metaphor that I can say have something to do with the path of initiation, where the hero must go into the underworld and wake up a mysterious maiden who will offer to him the mead of poetry, divine wisdom and immortality.

6. And then there is the story of Iðunn's abduction, which begins with three gods, Óðinn, Hænir and Loki, walking the young earth, and then starting something new, again.

But what IS that new thing they are creating?

I already suggested that it could have something to do with seiðr, shamanism and blót, that is, sacrifice. There is a staff involved, there is drumming involved, there is definitely something; sacrifice like - going on when the ox is being prepared in what is referred to as a seyði – an earth oven.

There are also three journeys to the other world involved; firstly, Loki, who is nearly taken over to the other side, so to speak, carried by a giant in eagle hide, who, as I discussed last time, may very well be a metaphor for mortality or death itself.

The second is Iðunn's journey, where she, a goddess of immortality, is abducted by the same eagle representing mortality and death – her very opposite.

The third is Loki's journey in the hide of a falcon – a hide that belongs to the goddess Freyia, who introduced the art of seiðr to gods and people, and which is also referred to as a Válshamr. Val is, as we know, also the term for those who are chosen for an eternally resurrecting life after death.

Loki brings Iðunn back, but with her appears what seems to be Iðunn's complete opposite; a dangerous giantess of injury, wolves and mountains, demanding justice and atonement for her loss; Skaði from Iron Forest. Today, we shall discuss the story in light of the older, poetic version; Haustlǫng, and see how kenningar and heiti – poetical metaphors and nicknames, may cast some light on the meanings and functions and identity of the characters involved.

THIÓÐOLF SKALD

The oldest source to the Iðunn myth that we have, the very one that Snorri based his prose tale on, is a skaldic poem known as Haustlǫng. It means something like the Prolonged Autumn. It was composed just before the year 900 by skald Thióðolf ór Hvini. Those of you who have read my Blade Honer series may recognize the name and profession of one important character, Thióðolf Skald. I would have loved to put the real Thióðolf Skald in this role, but the Thióðolf Skald of my novels lived almost a hundred years before the historical Thióðolf Skald, and I have made my fictional character Thióðolf into the grandfather of the historical Thióðolf, from whom the latter learned a lot about poetry. The last name – or what appears to be the last name; ór Hvini, means that the historical Thióðolf was from a place called Hvini.

It is believed that this place name is the same as Kvina in the district of Agder, south Norway, where we know that the Oseberg women dwelled for the last decades of their lives, and where the Oseberg ship was constructed. Thióðolf was not only known for where he was from, but also for his vast knowledge and wisdom; he was referred to as "hinn Fróði" – the wise. That is, Thióðolf the Wise.

Thióðolf ór Hvini
(ca.855-930 A.D.)

Norwegian Skald who lived during the Viking Age and who is most known for his two materpieces: Ynglingatál and Haustlǫng

Statue by Ståle Kylling-stad

Thióðolf lived right in the midst of the deep pagan Viking Age period. He was probably born around 850 and probably died before 930. He appears to have been closely connected to the Ynglinga kings. He served as skald to both Ragnvald Heiðumheri and to his ambitious cousin, Harald Hárfagri. Hárfagri means the one with the beautiful hair, also translated as Hair-Fair, although that translation suggests his hair was of fair color, while the meaning is actually "beautiful". The nickname did not exist in Harald's and Thióðolf's lifetimes, but was applied by later chroniclers who wanted to portray the first king of Norway in a favorable light.

In his own days, and while Thióðolf lived, king Harald was known as Harald Luva, which means Harald with the tangled hair, a reference to his refusal to comb and cut his hair until he had become king of all the Norwegian tribes. This resulted in natural dreadlocks and a nickname that later chroniclers thought unfit for the first king of our nation.

Harald managed to unite the tribes of Norway beneath his authoritarian sovereignty roughly back in the year 872. As a consequence, lots of former chiefs and tribal kings and their families fled to Iceland and, rather than fighting over who should be king of this new land, introduced what is now the oldest living democracy that still exist in Europe, the Icelandic parliament. Thióðolf, on the other hand, was but a poet who served at the court of this most powerful king that Norway had ever seen, and was clearly also connected to Harald's cousin, Ragnvald Heiðumheri, who had used to be the king of Vestfold, and the last of the Ynglinga dynasty.

Now, the Ynglinga dynasty ended their days in Vestfold, Norway, but they began over in Sweden a thousand years earlier, at least according to their own family history. How do we know their family history? Well. Ragnvald Heiðumheri and Harald Hárfagri both descended from these Ynglingar, and they could count their lineage back from son to father for 30 generations. In their family line, they could name 30 kings and their relatives and important events during their era of kingship, as well as how each one died.

We do not know if these stories are true, but since the poem was addressed to a living descendant who must have known his own royal lineage stories well, we know that people back then, in the late 9th century, deep Viking Age, certainly believed that these stories of royal and divine descent were true. And: To be able to count a lineage back for 30 generations is bloody impressive, my friends. 30 generations equals at least a thousand years. Since the poem was made some time before 900 AD, it takes us back to the first or second century BC, a different age altogether.

To be able to count your lineage back a thousand years is actually quite spectacular, even though it is only to be expected that when we reach back to the first kings, we have also reached back to a mythical past where the gods walked the earth and became to progenitors of royal dynasties. The Ynglingar seriously believed that they were descended from the god Freyr and the giantess Gerd.

Now, some time after 872 and probably before 900, Thióðolf was commissioned by Ragnvald Heiðumheri to make a poem about the Ynglinga lineage, preserving this family history of thirty generations forever after. Thióðolf composed a masterpiece that was known as the Ynglingatál – the counting of the Ynglingar. The poem names each king and how he died, basically.

Snorri made sure to preserve the poem and added to it in what has been known as the Ynglinga saga; where Snorri tells the tales of each king, tales that are only hinted at in the poem. The Ynglinga saga now constitutes the first saga of Snorri's Heimskringla, the sagas of the Norwegian kings. It is followed by the saga of Halfdan the Black, Harald Hair-Fair, Eirik Bloodaxe, and then of the three Christian kings whose ruling periods, eventually, after a century of efforts, finally led to the conversion of Norway in 1030.

But let us go back to Thióðolf. He died a century before there were any such attempts at Christian conversion. He composed his poetry to pagan kings, to a pagan audience, and was himself a pagan like everybody else during his time in Norway. While he is most famous for his Ynglingatál, he is also the poet behind another masterpiece; the Haustlǫng.

A SHIELD POEM

A Shield Poem is:

-A poem which describes the illustrations painted on a shield, in this case, a shield given to the skald Thióðolf by a man named Thorleif.

-The poem opens with an expression of gratitude for the named man - thus his name would live on in poetry.

In the year 900 Thióðolf visited a guy called Thorleif. For some reason, Thorleif gifted Thióðolf with a beautiful, painted shield, and the paintings on the shield described mythical scenes. In gratitude to Thorleif, Thióðolf composed a poem about the stories on the shield. These kinds of poems were known as shield poems, skiǫldkvíður. Ok, let me explain what a shield poem is. As said, Haustlǫng is described as a so called skiǫldkvíða – a "shield poem". It means that the poem is made about an image painted on a shield, an image that the skald was observing while making a poem about it. On the shield were two paintings, illustrating two different myths; the first image was an illustration to the myth about Iðunn's abduction, and the second image was an illustration to the myth about Thor's battle with Hrungnir.

It was common for skalds to make poems about artwork that they were observing. In the Laxdæla saga, we find a description of how this could happen. There was a huge wedding party, and at the party, they were also going to initiate a new guest house. The guest house had been covered with paintings about mythical themes. The skald Ulfr Uggason composed a poem about the images in the new house, a poem called Húsdrápa, the House Song, and, incidentally, the poem tells an archaic, Viking Age version of myths such as Thor's journey to Hýmir and how he fished the Midgard-serpent, Baldr's funeral, and an otherwise unknown myth about how Heimdallr and Loki fight over Freyia's necklace in the shapes of seal and walrus.

In the case of the Haustlǫng, the images are painted on a shield, and the poem describes the imagery and the mythical contexts. We shall focus only on the first part of the poem, where Thióðolf tells his version of the Iðunn-myth – our oldest version. Skaldic poetry is composed in a fixed, poetical style that one cannot just change, so the poems have been kept exactly as they were first composed – they are windows right into the minds of humans who lived in this time and place. And it proves, among other things, that the Iðunn-myth was well known back then.

STANZA 1: INTRODUCTIONS

The first stanza begins with Thióðolf's expression of gratitude to the one who gave him the painted shield:

1. Hvé skalk góðs at gjǫldum gunnveggjar brú leggja -- -- -- -- -- -- raddkleif at Þórleifi. Týframra sék tíva trygglaust of far þriggja á hreingǫru hlýri hildar fats ok Þjaza.	1.How can I repay the Provider of the War-Wall's Bridge (the shield)? I received a well-decorat-ed Bridge of the Voice-Cliff (shield) from Thorleif. I see upon the shining Bat-tle-Sheet's (the shield's) ridge: Three divinely powerful gods, and Thiazi, in an uncertain situation.

As you can see here, the shield is never directly referred to as a shield. It is referred to in poetical metaphors; like the Well-Decorated Bridge of the Voice-Cliff, and the Bridge of the War-Wall, and the Battle Sheet's Ridge.

One of these poetical metaphors are extended to cover two different things: The War-Wall Bridge means the shield, but it is extended into the Provider of the War-Wall-Bridge, which means Thorleif, who gave the shield away. These are called kenningar, that by which something is known. A kenning means that you are applying completely different words into riddles that say something about what we are actually referring to, without saying it directly. Understanding this is the key to Old Norse poetry and, incidentally, to Old Norse mythology.

HEITI

In 1225, that is, more than 300 years after Thióðolf composed his poem about the Iðunn myth, Snorri sat down to explain what we now know as kenningar and heiti in Norse poems and myths. His work was called the Younger Edda or the Prose Edda. In order to explain the metaphors of Edda and skaldic poetry, he wrote down simplified, prosaic versions of the myths that are found in these poems. This has made it incredibly much easier to understand the myths and not the least the heiti and the kenningar that were applied.

In Norse skaldskáp, that is, the art of poetry, the art of saying one single thing in endless variation of words the very key to the art. Adding to the complicated kenningar where one uses a whole sentence to describe a character or thing, there are heiti, which are single-word cover names or nicknames that apply to and describe certain characters. An Óðinsheiti is, for example, one of his many cover names, such as Grímr, Báleygr, Svafnir, Hár, Þrídi and so on – there are lots of heiti for this god, many of them are listed in an Edda poem called Grímnismál - but having many different heiti, as in cover names or nicknames, was also common for all the other gods and goddesses.

Sometimes, we think we have to do with two different characters, but the one is really just the same as the other, only going by a different heiti. I have noticed that the heiti used for the character in that particular situation tends to be relevant to the narrative context, a way of illustrating what aspect of that character is applied in the situation. Like when Óðinn chose to name himself Grim in the poem Grímnismál, it is because the heiti – the Óðinsheiti – Grim, means the Masked One, and in this particular context, Óðinn comes visiting incognito – he is indeed masked in this particular situation.

We have another story from Flateyjarbók where the goddess Freyia appears as a mighty magician, and she is here called Gǫndul, which means "magician". So when we look at what the heiti means, and in what situation it is applied rather than the so-called "real" name, we see that the choice of nickname is relevant to what role that character has in the stories. The nicknames really do mean something and say something about their owners. Snorri listed many nicknames particular to one deity, but others are not listed, and we have to figure out who is really behind by ourselves. and unless we are already aware of whose nickname it is, we must look to symbols, attributes, functions, relations, in order to determine what god or goddess or other character we are really speaking of.

Take the giantess Hyrrokkin, for example. She is described in detail by Snorri as a woman who rides a wolf and who has serpents for reins. An image of that sort of woman is found on a rune stone, so we know it is old and authentic. We also find other characters described in exactly the same fashion; the giantess Hyndla, for example, is a giantess wolf rider, and we find another unnamed one who is referred to as a fylgja and an omen of death.

Hyndla and Hyrrokkin and the unnamed Fylgja are most likely identical to one another due to shared attributes and functions, and so we can learn more about the one wolf-riding giantess of many names by comparing the information we have about each cover-name. Since we are talking about Iðunn, let us mention one of her heiti – an Iðunnarheiti: She is called Snótr, which means an eloquent, intelligent and wise woman. This says something about her function and role – and as we shall see, Iðunn seems to have more to do with intellectual qualities than with, say, fertility.

Kenningar

A kenning is, as opposed to the heiti, a whole sentence (where one may also use heiti). The kenning, that by which a thing is known, may consist of two or more words that also describe the character by applying heiti, associations, attributes, functions and descriptive words that allow us to recognize the character, and these cover names are also applied while relevant to the context. The god Thor, for example, is referred to by the kenning: the Crusher of Giants' Skulls, in a story where he does indeed crush jǫtunn skull.

What Snorri had noticed back in the 1220s, was that young people of his day, after two centuries of Christian influence, often had problems understanding the old, traditional art of poetry, because they no longer understood what which had been composed in a subtle, symbolic, allusive manner, and this because they no longer knew all the stories behind the metaphors, and it was no longer completely self-evident that they would understand who the Crusher of Jǫtunn Skulls was, when the name of Thor himself was not said directly. The entire Norse art of Skaldskáp was based on using metaphors, similes, and allusions. This is why Snorri laid it upon himself to sit down and write down as many myths he could manage, based on older written sources, written by people who had been alive or had parents who were alive during the pagan time period, and on the oral transmission of a very old woman whose father had been a pagan priest and a grown man before Christianity was introduced in Iceland.[21]

It would take a century before paganism was outlawed, so when Snorri started his work, paganism had been outlawed for about 120 years. That means a few generations, and means that many young people were starting to lose their connection to the tales of old – but many were still remembering, doing their best to record the old lore before it was too late. This is why we should all be extremely thankful to Snorri Sturluson, for without him and his likes, we would not have known crap about Norse mythology.

---

21 Snorri explains his source material in detail in the introduction to the Heimskringla

Almost the entire story that I just told you about the myth of Iðunn, Snorri's version, is closely and faithfully based on the Skaldic poem Haustlǫng, which is at least 300 years older than Snorri's version, and which we can state with complete confidence was created in the form we know it by a real pagan during the real pagan era, a skald whose poetry was based on a tradition of complex poetry reaching back beyond to the dawn of the language itself. And this poem contains a lot of interesting metaphors that tell us something about the gods and the goddess they are referring to.

I am now going to go through the entire poem and try to explain the kenningar that are applied. This way, we will understand a lot more about Iðunn than just the fact that she is associated to apples, fruits and nuts. We may also understand more about the myth of Iðunn and what it may really mean, if we take the kenningar seriously as meaningful additions to the myth. The first stanza was, as we already mentioned, a celebration of gratitude from Thióðolf to Thorleif as a thanks for the beautiful, painted shield. We already mentioned the three different kenningar used to describe the shield itself, and how one of these was extended into a kenning for Thorleif, who gave the shield. The first stanza also introduces Thiazi, who is referred to as traitorous, and the three divinely powerful gods. These are soon identified as the gods Óðinn, Loki and Hænir.

Snorri Sturluson's Prose Edda is actaully a teaching book for Skaldksap (poetry/poetical metaphors) which he wrote because he observed that young people (in the 1220s) had problems understanding old Skaldic poetry because they no longer understdood the metaphorical references.

"I let write this work (the Prose Edda) so that young students of skaldskap may better understand that which is subtly composed.
That is cunningly hidden in symnbols." Snorri Sturluson, Prose Edda

Image: Snorre Sturluson illustration by Christian Krogh from Heimskringla, 1899 edition

Haustlǫng Stanza 2: The Tellers of the Stories

From the second stanza, the myth that has been painted onto the shield is described.

2. Segjǫndum fló sagna
snótar ulfr at móti
í gemlis ham gǫmlum
glammi ó fyr skǫmmu;
settisk ǫrn, þars æsir,
ár (Gefnar) mat bǫ́ru
(vasa byrgi-Týr bjarga
bleyði vændr) á seyði.

2. The Eloquent Woman's (=
Iðunn) Wolf (=Thiazi)
flew with noise and
wing-flapping
for un-short (=very long)
time ago
To the Tellers of the Stories
(=Aesir/gods)
He (Thiazi) wore the age-old
shape
of the year-old (=eagle)
The Eagle sat, in the begin-
ning of time
Where the Aesir carried
nourishment to the seyði
(earth oven)
The Fortress-Týr (=Thiazi)
of the Gefn (=Providing
Woman)
of the Mountains (=Skaði/
the giantess)
was no soft coward.

The second stanza begins with a description of the jǫtunn, that is, the giant Thiazi, who is also a giant in eagle disguise. He is described as Snótar Ulfr – which means "the wolf of the eloquent woman." The eloquent woman is a one-word description or a heiti for the goddess Iðunn, and tells us that Iðunn is indeed a match to her husband Bragi, the god of poetry. She is defined by this name as an eloquent and knowledgeable woman. This is Thióðolf's first mention of the goddess – as a snótr, an eloquent and knowledgeable woman. Her "wolf" is Thiazi – but in this context, it does not mean that Iðunn keeps wolves like any other giantess – it means that he is her robber, the one who hunts her and abducts her, takes her away. Wolves are very often used in poetry in order to describe that which hunts you, kills you, or devours you.

Thiazi's name is also interesting here. It might derive from a verb; þiaza, which means to bind someone in slavery, to abduct or catch someone. Thiazi's entire identity is, in other words, based on his role in the myth, namely to be the one who tries to slave-bind the goddess Iðunn, whose role is defined as the eloquent and wise and knowledgeable female.

There is also mention of wing-flapping and the sound of winds – and this is important. We shall get back to that.

He flew for an 'unshort' time ago, which is a typical Norse understatement; it means that this happened a VERY LONG TIME AGO. And he flew to those who have been known as Segjandi Sagna – the ones who are telling the stories, the storytellers – and this is a kenning for the gods. The kenning refers to the fact that the gods are also called Song-Smiths (Ljóðasmiðir) and Spell-Smiths (Galdrasmiðir), and to tales that more than hint at a view of the world as a great story full of stories being told by the gods, and which comes to life and reality when they are being re-told.

We also learn that this happened ár - that means "in the beginning of time", in very old times. In one stanza, we find two declarations about this being so long ago that there can be no doubt; This is a myth of origins – of how something got started.

HAUSTLǪNG STANZA 3: VERY WISE CORPSE-THROWER

3. Tormiðluðr vas tívum
tálhreinn meðal beina;
hvat kvað hapta snytrir
hjalmfaldinn því valda;
margspakr of nam mæla
mǫ́r valkastar bǫ́ru
(vasat Hœnis vinr hǫ́num
hollr) af fornum þolli.

3. Partly Un-Blended Treason (=Thiazi) was late to start the Meal of the Gods The Helmet-Clad Giver of Eloquence to the bonds (=the gods) (=Óðinn) believed that someone was behind this. The Very Wise Seagull's Intestines' Corpse-Throw-er of the Waves (=Thiazi) talked from the Age-Old Tree (=Yggdrasill) Hænir's Friend (=Loki) did not like him well.

In the third stanza, we hear about how late the eagle started the cooking for the gods, and that Óðinn understood that someone was behind this, and that Loki was pissed off. Now, here you may see how a skaldic poem works compared to the prose version. If Snorri had not explained the story to us, we might never have figured out what was really happening.

But since Snorri did the marvelous work that he did, we know that the gods were trying to cook an ox in the seyði – that is, the earth oven, but that the ox will not cook, and this is because of the jǫtunn in eagle hide sitting up in the very old tree. We learn two new kenningar for Thiazi: he is called Partly Un-Blended Treason, which is really contraindicative and mysterious in itself, and later on, he is referred to as the very wise corpse-thrower who belongs to the seagull-intestines of the waves. Hard to explain that, except by pointing out that there seems to be a reference to death and mortality here.

The word for corpse-thrower is válkastar, and vál specifically refers to the chosen dead, those who have been chosen by the valkyriur to come to Valhalla, a sort of salvation in the form of eternal life and resurrection. So this is important: Thiazi is portrayed as someone who destroys the vál, who destroys what may lead to eternal life and resurrection. Óðinn is referred to as the helmet-clad giver of eloquence to the bonds, and bond is a heiti for «god». So Óðinn is the helmet-clad giver of eloquence to the gods. Have you all noticed that there is a theme of eloquence here? Eloquence as in poetry and knowledge.

Óðinn is defined as the divine origin of these qualities. And he is the one who realizes that Thiazi, the giant in eagle hide, is the one who obstructs their meal from cooking. Loki is referred to as Hænir's friend. Hænir is the one who gave the art of thinking to humankind, so this means that Loki is here defined as a fried of the mind, a friend of thoughts, or that which gives us mind and thoughts.

HAUSTLǪNG STANZA 4: THE RAVEN GOD'S FRIEND

4. Fjallgylðir bað fyllar
fet-Meila sér deila
(hlaut) af helgum skutli
(hrafnásar vinr blása);
ving-rǫgnir lét vagna
vígfrekr ofan sígask,
þars vélsparir vǫ´ru
varnendr goða farnir.

4. The Mountain-Howler
(the wolf = Thiazi)
asked The One Who
Ascends the Armour
(=Óðinn)
to share with him a part
of the Holy Meal *
The Raven-God's
(=Óðinn's) Friend
(=Loko)
had to blow the fire
The War-Hungry Ruler of
the Wagon of Friendship
(=Thiazi)
let himself descend from
above)
to where the Loyal Pro-
tectors of the Gods (=the
Aesir) had arrived.

Here we see Thiazi being called the Mountain-Howler. Howler is a known heiti for a wolf, and is a metaphor for who or what hunts you, whether it is your enemy who wants to take you down, or simply the power of mortality and death itself. Adding a Mountain to the heiti for wolf, now that is a simple kenning working as a heiti that indicates a giant.

Óðinn is referred to as the Raven God, and I assume we all know why, he owns two ravens called Húginn and Múninn, the thought and the memory. Loki is referred to as Óðinn's friend, and here, he is especially a friend to the qualities associated with Óðinn's ravens – thought and mind. This is the second time in this poem that Loki is identified as a friend of the mind.

Thiazi is later on referred to as the war-hungry ruler of the wagon of friendship – whatever that really means, and we learn that this ruler descends from above – from the top of the age-old tree, in order to take a part of the holy meal of the gods. The three Aesir gods, Óðinn, Loki and Hænir, are now referred to as the loyal protectors of the gods.

Before anyone objects to this unusual presentation, to this importance of an otherwise very little-known god such as Hænir, or to Loki being a friend to, and a loyal protector of, the gods, let me remind you that this is our oldest source to an actual Norse myth, and that it was composed in the form we know it during the Viking Age – a long time before the demonization of Loki into something that looks like a Satan figure. Here, Loki is problematic, but also ambivalent and very complex. His gifts to the gods are considerable.

HAUSTLǪNG STANZA 5: THE GODDESS OF THE DRUMMING BELT

5. Fljótt bað foldar dróttinn
Fárbauta mǫg Várar
þekkiligr með þegnum
þrymseilar hval deila,
en af breiðu bjóði
bragðvíss at þat lagði
ósvífrandi ása
upp þjórhluti fjóra.

5. The Virtuous Lord of
Earth (=Óðinn)
Immediately demanded
that
The Son of Fárbauti
(=Loki)
should divide
The Whale (=the ox) of
the Vár (=Alert Goddess)
of the Drumming Belt (=
Iðunn)
with the Serving Man
(=Thiazi)
And the Deed-Wise Dis-
turber of the Gods (=Loki)
now shared the ox in four
up on the Broad Table
(=the altar)

In the fifth verse, Óðinn is known as the virtuous lord of the earth, and he orders Loki to share the ox, which is suddenly referred to as the «Whale of the Goddess of the Drumming Belt". What this means and what it says about the dead ox or, perhaps, the sacrifice, is truly obscure. But the word for goddess used is Vár, who is listed by Snorri among the goddesses of Ásgarðr, and whose name means to be aware, that is, she represents awareness or alertness. According to Snorri, Vár is wise and quick of mind, she listens to oaths and deals, and avenges betrayal of oaths.

That she is used to represent the goddess of the drumming belt whose whale is the sacrificial meal is probably important. The theme of intelligence, thought, and awareness keeps being repeated in this poem. As is the theme of - drumming. Who is the goddess of the drumming belt? I assume she is the recipient of what could be the sacrifice, since the ox is dedicated to her.

What ox, you may ask, and I can only say welcome to the world of cover-words; I know it is odd, but just as a god could be mentioned by the name of another god, for as long as we provide a context that allows us to recognize who we are talking about, an animal could be used to describe another animal. The whale is no whale, but the ox, and it is common to say whale instead of ox in poetry, both animals being huge and heavy. So the ox, what might be the sacrifice, belongs to the mysterious goddess of the drumming belt- and who is that? Who is the one that the gods themselves sacrifice to?

It could, technically, be Iðunn, since she is the main goddess of this story. But the kenning, goddess of the drumming belt, does not make sense in any context that we know about (I think). This could have two explanations; there was once a myth in which Iðunn did have something to do with a drumming belt, or with whatever that drumming belt may be a metaphor for, but that myth is lost to us, so that we lack the context that would make the kenning meaningful as a metaphor for Iðunn.

The other explanation is that the kenning is referring to another character, and it is hard to know which one. The only thing that occurred to me is the fact that the lady of the dead, Hel, lives near a river called Giǫll, which means "the Resounding One", and to cross it, which means that you are entering the land of the dead, one has to cross a bridge called Gjallarbrú, the Resounding Bridge. This bridge is said to vibrate and resound. The drumming belt could very well be a kenning for this bridge to the other world, to the afterlife, and the goddess of that bridge could be Hel or any other female character associated with death

I mentioned sacrifice, that the meal could be a sacrifice, a blót. In this context, it is interesting that the ox is laid on a broad table, which could be a way of saying altar. We are speaking of a holy meal, a meal for the gods, a meal that is laid out on a table. We are very likely seeing a mythical description of the first sacrifice. In the Ynglinga saga, we learn that the Aesir were the ones who first practiced and then shared and taught the art of making sacrifice, so that the Aesir themselves are introducing this practice back in the dawn of time is very likely a major theme of this story.

Haustlǫng Stanza 6: The Hidden God of the Deep Soul

6. Ok slíðrliga síðan
svangr (vas þat fyr lǫngu)
át af eikirótum
okbjǫrn faðir Marnar,
áðr djúphugaðr dræpi
dolg ballastan vallar
hirði-Týr meðal herða
herfangs ofan stǫngu.

6. And The Hungry Father
(=Thiazi)
of the Giantess (=Skaði)
ate greedily from
the Tame Bear of the Oak
Roots (=the ox)
This was a long time ago –
Before The Hidden Beast
of the Deep Soul (=Loki)
hit the War-Trophy (=Thi-
azi) with his staff
He beat the Mighty Enemy
of Earth (=Thiazi)
from above, between the
shoulders.

In the sixth stanza, we learn that Thiazi eats too much from the ox, and that Loki beats him with his staff between his shoulders. Thiazi is referred to as the hungry father of the giantess, a direct hint to him being, as we know, the father of the giantess called Skaði. It is also pointed out that he is very hungry – he is, after all, the corpse-swallower himself.

He eats greedily of the ox, which is now referred to as the tame bear of the oaken roots, and it is once more pointed out that this happened a very long time ago. We also learn that Thiazi is a powerful enemy of Earth, that is, of our world, the world that the gods were starting to shape.

Loki is, weirdly enough, referred to as - the beast that hides deeply in the soul; interesting!

HAUSTLǪNG STANZA 7: THE GHOST OF THE GIANT WORLD

7. Þá varð fastr við fóstra
farmr Sigvinjar arma,
sás ǫll regin eygja,
ǫndurgoðs, í bǫndum;
loddi rǫ´ við ramman
reimuð Jǫtunheima,
en holls vinar Hœnis
hendr við stangar enda.

7. Then was The Burden of
Sígyn's Arms (=Loki)
- he whom all the gods per-
ceive as chained
bound and fastened to the
Foster-Father (=Thiazi) of the
Skiing Goddess (=Skaði)
His Staff was glued
to the Ghost of the Giant
World (=Thiazi)
And the hands of Hænir's
Loyal Friend (=Loki)
Was glued to the staff.

In the seventh stanza, we learn that Loki is glued to his staff, and that the staff is glued to Thiazi. Loki is referred to by his relation to his wife, Sígyn – to say that someone is a burden of someone else's arms is a way of saying that they sleep together or are married. Thiazi is referred to by his relation to his daughter, who he fosters, his daughter being Ǫndurdís – the skiing goddess. This is another way of saying Skaði. As soon as the staff is glued, Thiazi is referred to as a ghost of the giant world – one who is now dead, which makes sense since he dies in this myth, but it is also another way of alluding to the theme of mortality and death in this story.

Haustlǫng Stanza 8: The Vulture of the Flock

8. Fló með fróðgum tívi
fangsæll of veg langan
sveita nagr, svát slitna
sundr ulfs faðir mundi;
þá varð Þórs of-rúni
(þungr vas Loptr of
sprunginn)
mǫ´ lunaut, hvat's mátti,
miðjungs friðar biðja.

8. The Vulture of the Flock
(=Thiazi)
was happy with his catch
and flew far away with the
knowledgeable God (=Loki)
so that the Wolf's Father
(=Loki)
was about to be torn asunder.
Then Thor's Friend (=Loki)
begged for mercy from
The Child of the Jǫtunn
(=Thiazi)
For all his power, The Heavy
Air (=Loki)
was about to break down.

In the eight stanza, Thiazi is known as the Vulture of the Flock. A vulture is another animal clearly associated to death and mortality – a vulture feeds on the dead, after all. In the flock – perhaps the flock of participants in this story – Thiazi represents that which feeds on death, mortality itself. Loki is here called the Wise God, the Fróðr Tív. Fróðr means that he is wise, knowledgeable and cunning too.

He is also referred to by his relations; as the father of the wolf and the friend of the god Thor. All this in the same stanza. Oh, and there is one more: When Loki begs for mercy, he is called thungr Loptr - The Heavy Air. Loptr is, by the way, a common heiti for Loki, and does indeed mean air.

HAUSTLQNG STANZA 9: THE STIRRER OF THE STORIES & THE GODDESS OF THE BENCHES OF THE WATER-SOURCE-FIELDS

<table>
<tr>
<td>

9. Sér bað sagna hrœri
sorgœran mey fœra,
þás ellilyf ása,
áttrunnr Hymis, kunni;
Brunnakrs of kom bek-
kjar
Brísings goða dísi
girðiþjófr í garða
grjót-Níðaðar síðan.

</td>
<td>

9. Hýmir's Lineage Tree
(=Thiazi) asked
The One Who Stirs the Sto-
ries (=Loki)
- who was crazy from pain -
If he (Loki) could bring to
him (Thiazi)
The Wonderful Maiden who
Knows the Age-Cure of the
Aesir (=Iðunn)
The Belt-Thief of the Flaming
Gods (=Loki)
then brought
The Goddess of the Fields of
the Water-Sources (=Iðunn)
To the farms of the Rock-Rul-
er Below (=Thiazi)

</td>
</tr>
</table>

In the ninth stanza, Thiazi is known as the Lineage Tree of Hýmir. This is a way of knowing Thiazi through his relations, in this case his relation to the lineage tree of the jǫtunn Hýmir. This giant, Hýmir, is the very same who helped Thor fish up the Midgard-serpent in another story, while Thor is on a quest for a cauldron worthy of being filled with the sacred mead of the gods.

The poet could have used any giant to illustrate relationship to another giant, but he chose Hýmir, and thus gives us an allusion to the myth of Hýmir or to whatever else Hýmir represents. That is probably not coincidental, but we would have to make a great detour around the myth of Hýmir and Thor in order to explain it, and that would take too much time, so I will leave this matter of a possible connection between the themes to another time.

In this stanza, Loki is known Sagna Hrærir, the one who moves the stories. This is a wonderful image of how Loki's role in mythical narratives is to create conflict and drama, what actually moves an event into a story worth telling. Loki is also known as the Belt-Thief of the Flaming Gods, which may be an allusion to the story we only know from Flateyjarbók and the skaldic poem Húsdrápa, in which Loki must steal Freyia's necklace on behalf of another passionate god; Óðinn himself.

We have also talked about belts before – this does not have to refer to the same so-called belt, which turned out to possibly refer to the resounding bridge of Hel, but it could be. In that case, Loki "steals" the bridge of death in some way, a good, poetical description of how Loki in this poem does indeed conquer death. This is the first stanza that really mentions Iðunn.

Thiazi calls her the Wonderful Maiden who knows the age-cure of the Aesir, alluding to her role as the one who resurrects and renews the gods so that they may stay young and live forever – their divine immortality is completely dependent on this goddess, so even if she has hardly been mentioned up to now, she is in truth extremely important to the gods.

They would not exist as gods without her, they would have grown old and died like any other mortal. She is the source to their divinity. Thiazi also calls her the goddess of the benches of the fields of the water-springs. Now what field are these? Fields full of water-springs? A field where the flows of water originate?

This is a place of origin, the place where the rivers and streams of the world are springing out from. There are benches here, which means that some may find their seats here, and Iðunn is the goddess of those seats. The one who decides who to get to stay in this strange realm of water welling up from their point of ultimate origins.

I have not discussed Iðunn's proper name yet. Her name derives, probably, **from iða**, which means, exactly, a water stream. But not just any water stream, it is the sort of stream which turns around and starts flowing back in the direction of its origin. A bit like an eddy - a circular movement of water causing a small whirlpool. A spirally design occurs, as the stream attempts to return to its origin, but is steadily influenced by the movement of the main stream.

Do you get it now?

I will give you a hint. There are <u>many places </u>in Ásgarðr, such as Urðarbrunnr, the Well of Origin, where the norns dwell, shaping our destiny, and where they water and renew the universe every day from their water-spring. As I have told you before, one thing, one character and one place may appear by numerous different names. So let me tell you now, that there is also a place in Ásgarðr known as the Iðavǫllr.

The name may be connected to the same word for eddy, in which case this is also a place of river stream whirlpools attempting to get back to their sources.There may be other words that have influenced the name too, such as iðuliga, which means continual, suggesting that this is a place that continues or is renewing itself continuously - and this is also another possible explanation for the name Iðunn.

There have been other suggestions as to meanings, such as the Splendid Fields or the Field of Activity, but if we look to the context of where and when Iðavǫllr is mentioned, but since we have a kenning for Iðunn that definitely refers to a field of water-stream-sources, I am pretty convinced that the meaning of an eddy, a stream turning back towards its source, creating a spiral whirlpool, is the original meaning of the name.

The place Iðavǫllr is clearly a place of renewal and starts and the origin of "streams" – <u>streams being symbolic of something like life and movement</u>. The Iðavǫllr is a part of Ásgarðr that is destined to survive Ragnarǫk. Here, the divine survivors, the children of the gods who died during Ragnarǫk, will gather after the apocalypse and begin the world once more. I am pretty sure that Iðunn and Iðavǫllr are deeply connected, since new life in the form of resurrection from death and renewal of youth, does spring from her and her only. This is where Fate starts.

Do you get it now?

Haustlǫng Stanza 10: The Gods Are Ageing

<table>
<tr><td>

10. Urðut brattra barða
byggvendr at þat hryg-
gvir;
þá vas Ið með jǫtnum
unnr nýkomin sunnan;
gættusk allar áttir
Ingvifreys at þingi
(vǫ´ru heldr) ok hárar
(hamljót regin) gamlar.

</td><td>

10. The Residents of the Steep
Mountains (iotnir/giants)
were not very sad (=were
overjoyed)
That Iðunn had come from
the south (=Ásgarðr)
All of Yngvi-Freyr's Lineages
(=the gods)
- ageing and grey of hair -
went to parliament
The Rulers (=gods)
were rather ugly to look at
now.

</td></tr>
</table>

In the tenth stanza, we learn that the giants, or as they are known; the Residents of the Steep Mountains, are not very sad when Iðunn arrives from the south. The south means Ásgarðr, which is situated in the south of the world, where the norns also dwell, and Iðunn comes from this direction. That the giants are not very sad is an example of typical Norse understatement humor. It means that they are super-happy about it.

But it was different in Ásgarðr. There, all the lineages of Yngvi Freyr, that is, all the gods, Aesir and Vanir and elves and any other being who had reached divine status, were aging, gray-haired, and ugly to look at by the time they painstakingly managed to gather for parliament.

It was the parliament that rules the universe, the parliament of all the gods and goddesses together. It is frequently mentioned in Edda poetry. The parliament is always held by the Well of Origin, and they will all gather there whenever something of major importance for the world – or for all the worlds – was at stake, such as the fact that they had become mortal and were aging and dying because their goddess, Iðunn, had vanished. This is a story about the loss of their most important goddess, and what that loss means for the gods. Without her, they will wither and die.

HAUSTLǪNG STANZA 11: THE PRECIOUS MAIDEN WHO INCREASES THE JOY OF THE GODS

11. Unz hrynsæva hræva hund ǫlgefnar fundu leiðiþirr ok læva lund ǫlgefnar bundu; þú skalt véltr, nema, vélum, - vreiðr mælti svá - leiðir mun stœrandi mæra mey aptr, Loki, hapta.	11. Until they (the gods) found The Flowing Corpse-Sea's Blood-Hound (=Loki) of the Beer-Gefn (=Iðunn) and bound the thief, The Tree of Betrayal (=Loki) who had led The Beer-Pro- vider (=Iðunn) astray. «You shall suffer terribly, Loki,» Thus spoke The Angry One (Thor?) «unless you bring back The Precious Maiden Who Increases the Joy of the Gods (=Iðunn)

In the eleventh stanza, Loki is brought to court, bound and ordered to make Iðunn come back to them. Iðunn is here known by the heiti Ǫlgefn, which means the Beer Provider, she who gives us the drink. Those of you who are familiar with my work on the Maiden with the Mead may raise an eyebrow here, as would I. Is Iðunn the "real" Maiden with the Mead? Is she the one behind all the other cover names of goddesses, valkyriur, giantesses and norns who guard the precious mead in a bright realm within the darkest depths of death?

The source of poetry, inspiration, knowledge, wisdom, and, of course, immortality in the form of resurrection from death - through the ritual drinking and the union with the mead-woman? Could she be? Of course she could be. But it has to be said that other female characters are also referred to as beer-providers. Thióðolf himself gave exactly the same title to another character later on in the poem, when he tells the tale of how Thor went to fight against Hrungnir. I will not be rendering this part of the poem here, because it is another story, but the story ends with a vǫlva – a witch named Gróa - arriving to heal Thor from a battle wound by the use of galdrar – spell-songs.

And here, Gróa is also referred to as Ǫlgefn, the Beer Provider. So the use of this heiti may obviously be shared by several different or at least apparently different characters. It could possibly just mean a very generous, nurturing woman who brings something wonderful to the thirsty man, like Gróa brings healing to the injured Thor. And it could mean both. Loki is now Ǫlgefn's, or Iðunn's bloodhound of the flowing corpse sea. A bloodhound is one who tracks something, so Loki is now tracking Iðunn, clearly. It could also mean that he is her enemy in this poem, at least when he helps give her over to the giants.

The flowing corpse sea may be an allusion to what his action has caused: death, a lot of death. So he is also called the Tree of Betrayal, and he is bound. This is another myth of how Loki is bound and punished in some way, I believe there are three such stories. One is when he gets his mouth sewn together despite bringing wonderful gifts to the gods, all because he lost a bet to a dwarf, another is when he is revealed to be behind the death of Baldr. This is the oldest story we know for certain, where Loki is bound by the aging gods because of his role in the abduction of Iðunn. The gods demand that Loki make amends and saves the day by bringing back the Wonderful Maiden who Increases the Joy of the Gods.

HAUSTLQNG STANZA 12: CHILD OF THE HAWK AND LOVER OF GODS

<table>
<tr><td>

12. Heyrðak svá, þat
(síðan
sveik opt ǫ́su leikum)
hugreynandi Hœnis
hauks fló bjalfa aukinn,
ok lómhugaðr lagði
leikblaðs reginn fjaðrar
ern at ǫglis barni
arnsúg faðir Marnar.

</td><td>

12. I have heard this, that
Hænir's Intent-Tester (=Loki)
later lured back
The Lover of the Gods
(=Iðunn)
He flew away in the shape of
the Hawk

And the Father of the Giant
Woman
 (=Thiazi, Skaði's father),
that Fast, Wing-Flapping
King-Tricker (=Thiazi)
followed, with Eagle-Suction
(=wind/ death/
mortality)
after the Hawk's Child
(=Loki)

</td></tr>
</table>

In the twelfth stanza, we learn that Loki brings back the goddess. Loki is now called Hænir's Intent-Tester, that is, the one who tests the intentions or will of the thoughts. He lures back Iðunn, who is now referred as Ása Leika – which directly means that she is the one lover of all the gods. He flew away in the shape of a falcon, which can be used interchangeably with hawk, and is therefore called Child of the Hawk. He is followed by the fast, wing-flapping king-tricker, that is, Thiazi, and he is followed with arnsug – that is, "eagle suction" - the swallowing gape of the eagle, or the suction power of the eagle, the winds of the eagle, as before mentioned; he is being followed by Death, by Mortality itself.

Haustlǫng Stanza 13: In Suddenness His Journey Ended

13. Hófu skjótt, en skófu,
skǫpt, ginnregin, brinna,
en sonr biðils sviðnar
(sveipr varð í fǫr) Grei-
par.
Þat's of fátt á fjalla
Finns ilja brú minni.
Baugs þák bifum fáða
bifkleif at Þórleifi.

13. The wooden poles that the
Sacred Rulers (the gods) had
turned into timber began to
burn
And the Son of He Who Loves
Greipr (=Thiazi)
also burnt
- Abruptly, his journey ended.

I received the border's mov-
ing cliff (=the shield)
decorated with horrors, from
Thorleif.

In the thirteenth stanza, we hear that the timber begins to burn, a special wood that the Ginnregin, the sacred rulers, had made into a pyre. And all too suddenly did his life end, Thiazi, now known as the one who was the son of the giant who loved the giantess Greipr. *Greipr means The Gripping One, a giantess, here presented as Thiazi's mother. In Skaldskaparmál, she is the giant Geirrǫð's daughter, able to piss a whole river, while in the Edda poem Hyndluljóð, she is one of the nine mothers of Heimdall – the Great World. We do not get to hear the story about Skaði, for here, Thióðolf turns his attention to the next illustration painted onto his shield, and begins the tale of Thor's journey to meet the giant Hrungnir and how he was healed by Gróa. We will leave the Haustlǫng for now, and look to what it all may mean.

The Three Gods

Let us go back to start, to the three powerful gods and Thiazi's traitorous coming in-between. Firstly we are introduced to the three gods; Óðinn, Loki and Hænir. As I mentioned before, we have several origin myths involving three gods on a journey. From the Edda poem Vǫluspá, we have the myth of how Óðinn, Víli and Vé emerge while the young universe is still in a state of chaos, and give shape to the world.

We could say that the three gods represent Spirit, Intent and Sacred Space. Why? Óðinn's name derives from Óðr, which means poetry, inspiration and ecstasy. Óðinn also gives andr to human beings; andr means both breath and spirit. For this reason, I think it is meaningful to say that Óðinn is THE spirit. The name of his brother, Vé, means a sacred location, a shrine or a temple or, simply, sacred space. The name of his brother Víli literally translates as will, as in intent. So the blueprint for the formula of the three gods who cause important cosmic changes, are Spirit, Intent and Sacred Space, and the latter could possibly be a way saying the mind.

The formula is repeated in Norse myths, and I think they all reflect on the same original trinity of Spirit, Intent and Mind. When the gods walk the earth and decide to create humankind, we have the trio Óðinn, Hænir and Hlóðurr. Óðinn offers andr, that is, he offers breath and spirit. Hænir offers Óðr, which is exactly the same word that is used to make the name Óðinn. However, it is clear that Hænir offers thought and mind to humankind. Hlóðurr is a god not otherwise mentioned, which means that we are speaking of a heiti – a cover name. The heiti means "Heat" or "glow" or "The Heating" or "The Glowing One", and what he gives to humankind is the spark of life itself, and líta góða - many beautiful colors.

Later on, we are presented with a third version of this original trinity, where Óðinn and Hænir stay the same, while Hlóðurr is replaced with Loki. This is the trinity we meet in the Haustlǫng, our oldest source to such a trinity, and the same trinity is also found in a different Edda story. It looks to me like Óðinn remains Óðinn, the breath giver, the spirit giver in all the versions. Vé, the sacred space, seems to correspond with Hænir, the one who gives mind and thought, while Hlóðurr and Víli correspond with Loki; the one who gives life-spark and color to the stories, the one of will and intent and passionate heat.

Hænir's name is very strange, because it simply means chicken, in plural. Like lots of chicken clucking and plucking about, and I have never been able to see this meaning as anything else but humor, an ironic way of describing thoughts and words and poetry itself, as something that does indeed incessantly cluck away, and plucking and picking up everything it sees. Hlóðurr, of whom we know very little otherwise, means the Glowing One, and he is the one who gives to the people vitality, the force of life, and many beautiful colors, and who corresponds to Loki and Víli in the other trinities we are presented with.

> **To sum up:** So there is one story explaining how the world assembled in its present order, beginning with a trinity. There is a second story explaining how humankind became gifted by the gods, beginning with a trinity.

There is a third myth, which we find in the Edda poem Reginsmál. This is when the Red Gold and with it, the ring of Andvari, are discovered, and lost, and coveted by Óðinn ever after. The ring of Andvari is interesting; the name Andvari is derived from andr: spirit /breath and vari: alert, aware, guard. One could almost think it had something to do with breath awareness or an alert, aware spirit. The ring might be identical to the ring Draupnir. Draupnir has that quality, that it drips nine new rings exactly like itself every ninth night, which is obviously metaphorical for something.

In another myth, we learn that when Balder is laid on the funeral pyre, Óðinn leaves that ring with him, so the ring went into Hel together with Balder, into the underworld. Then a hero called Hermóðr had to ride the resounding bridge of Hel in order to try and rescue Balder from Hel, but he cannot get Balder back to the world of the living – only the self-rejuvenating ring. The ring and the red gold is linked to a path of initiation that is described throughout the poems that follow; the hero Sigurd must take the Red Gold away from the poisonous serpent who wears the Helmet of Terror, and then he must carry the Red Gold in order to reach and wake his sleeping Valkyria, so that she may teach him the true power of runes, drink the mead of universal memory, and learn how to heal with his hands.

In this story of the Red Gold, we have the same trio that we know about from Haustlǫng: We have Óðinn, Hænir and a replacement for Hlóðurr – or for Víli: Loki. There is a myth in which Loki is paired with a giant called Lógi, which means the flame, and Hlóðurr, whose place Loki takes, means the glowing one. Loki is the one who gives action and drama and conflict to the stories – he is the Sagna Hrærir, the stirrer of the stories – and it is only suitable that he overlaps with an otherwise obscure god whose mission is to offer the gift of vitality, life-force and colors to human beings.

Maybe this is, ultimately, what Loki represents and why his role is so ambivalent – he is that beast hiding deep in the souls of people, not good nor bad, not god nor giant, a being in between worlds, born jǫtunn but turned god through mixing his blood with Óðinn in times of origin. In Norse myths, the number three is associated with change and creation, the beginning of something new, whether it be the three gods who shape the world and offer gifts of spirit and mind, the three norns who write down the laws and determine all fate, or the three giantesses who demand that the dwarfs be made, so that the gods may enter the world through their forms, as it is said in the Vǫluspá.

Most myths explain the origin of something; important divine actions that paved the ground for the order of the world and important rituals that humans must attend to. Such as shamanic spirit travels and sacrifice. In other words: The journey of the three gods at the beginning of time is a repeated theme, a sort of formula that keeps popping up in the myths and which, each time, explain the origin of something, such as a holy action that was central to their religion. If you wonder what sort of ritual was the most central to Old Pre-Christian, Scandinavian religion, I would immediately say that both blot, as in sacrifice, and seiðr, were central to their religion. It is only natural that there would be a myth of origin for both things. What is interesting is how they seem to come together, as if sacrifice and seiðr are ultimately and deeply connected to each other.

Blót

And herein lies an important point: I believe that the Iðunn myth is no fertility myth at all, but rather a myth about how blot and shamanic out-of-body travels to other worlds, and to the world of death itself, came to be. And also, incidentally, about what it means on a deeper level. It has to do with divinity, with the quest for knowledge and immortality- through such ritual acts. In the Haustlǫng poem, we learn that the ox – a typical sacrificial beast – as laid in the seyði, the earth oven. As mentioned before, the seyði is not identical to seiðr, but may be a linguistic, poetic allusion to the same, while also determining that this sacrifice is happening within the spheres of the earth.

Whether it has something to do with seiðr or not, we know that the ox was placed in an earth oven called a seyði, and that it was supposed to cook there. Loki, who is often called Loptr, which means air, must blow hard on the fire. It is Loki who is the active part in the whole story, despite his ambivalence he is the protagonist of the whole thing. Loki being the active part is significant. Loki is a great performer of seiðr. He can shape-change, and shape-change he does; he becomes fly and otter and seal and salmon and woman too, he frequently borrows Freyia's falcon hide in order to travel between dimensions, and if there is anything Loki is an expert of, it is travel between realities.

He is also different from the other gods; he was born a jǫtunn and became an áss, as in a god, by blending his blood with Óðinn. Like a human shaman or priest archetype, he achieves divinity through his blending with a god. His gifts the gods with magical things, and like a proper seiðr-man who could also be a woman at the same time, he gives birth to Sleipnir, a magical horse that can travel unharmed through the realms of death; Óðinn and some human heroes have performed this act of traveling to death and back with the help of Loki's gift. And this story, my friends, of how Loki almost died and then had to go right into the death he feared so in order to rescue the goddess, is perhaps his first journey as a shaman type, perhaps this is his initiation.

But seiðr and shamanism is not the only theme here. It is strongly connected to another important. Pagan ritual form: Blót – sacrifice. The story may very well tell us about the origins of blót. As we know from other sources, the Aesir gods were big on sacrifice, they received it as gods, and it is said that when they walked the earth like human beings and became progenitors of royal dynasties all over the place, they were the first blótgóðir – the first sacrificial priests. Also, Freyia, who is known for being the first and ultimate teacher of seiðr – the one who offers her falcon hide to Loki, is also known to be a blótgyðja – a sacrificial priestess. It is very likely that blot and seiðr goes together like hand in glove.

Let us look back to the story, where the ox is placed on the broad table, which of course may be a description of a large stone altar. The meal is then called «helgi skutl» - the holy meal. It is also referred to as «the meal of the gods». This clearly does indicates a sacrifice and the sacrificial meal – the ones that the gods shall receive when they enter the realms of the earth, and which they prepared themselves for the very first time, staking out a path of ritual for humans to follow. So, as I mentioned earlier on, there is a staff involved, which could be an indication of an act of seiðr – it is in fact the staff that makes it possible for Loki to travel between worlds in the first place – the staff is stuck to the eagle and carries Loki away.

He gets frightened and offers up – well he could as well have offered up his soul to the eagle of death when he offers up Iðunn, but he is panicked. Later, he applies Freyia's falcon hide in order to travel between the worlds, but the first time was with a staff, and may be an indication of seiðr. As I also said before, Another possible hint towards a shamanic variant of seiðr is the fact that Thiazi's abode is in Þrýmheimr, and that this alludes to a world ruled by drumming, steady beat vibrations – a typical feature of shamanic séance rituals.

Hyndluljóð

Do we have other myths that could clarify the connection between seiðr and blót, or between blót and the act of traveling into other worlds associated with great mortal danger?

Yes we do!

The Edda poem Hyndluljóð begins with an act of blót, and act of sacrifice. The hero, Óttarr, makes blot to the goddesses, and sacrifices a boar. The blood runs down the stone altar, and the stone turns into crystal. Then the goddess Freyia appears, turns Óttarr into the dying boar, and rides him down int the underworld. In other words, by the grace of the great goddess, Óttarr's spirit has merged with the boar he just killed, and he is now on his way into the underworld, steered by the goddess. Down there, in the darkest depths of darkness, they meet a wolf-riding giantess vǫlva called Hyndla, which means she-wolf or just bitch, and she keeps a stable full of male wolves that she rides at her pleasure. Freyia still addresses her as «sister» and as «maiden among maidens", invoking her, waking her up.

She begs of Hyndla that she teaches Óttarr about his lineage, so that Óttarr may return to the land of the living with new knowledge that he will need in his fight against Angantýr – a name which, by the way, happens to mean: **The God of Pleasure**. Óttarr sort of has to fight the god of pleasure like any other monk, and he has to fight it with deep knowledge gathered from the lady who rules the underworld. It turns out that the secret to understanding Óttarr's lineage is to understand that it is a lineage of the entire world, all lineages that ever came out of Heimdallr, the splendid world itself. He is a kinsman to gods, elves, giants, trolls, and all sorts of human lineages – they are all your kind, says Hyndla, Óttarr heimski-heimski means; of the narrow mind. She is evidently trying to expand his mind and realize his deep interconnectedness with ALL lineages of the universe.

In order to remember all that he has learned in this unusual state of perception, Freyia offers him what she called the Drink of Memory and calls upon all the gods to help Óttarr. There is more to the story what we might discuss in another lecture, but the point here is really that Óttarr travels between dimensions and enters the underworld, learning things from two female characters who are clearly masters of seiðr itself, and all this is so that he might reach Valhalla – a state of immortality after death. He manages this feat by performing - an act of sacrifice, a blot to the goddess. And the real magic of traveling between the worlds happens when his soul merges with the sacrifice – he journeys WITH the dying boar right down into the underworld.

The **<u>sacrificer becomes, in other words, the sacrifice</u>**, it is by its blood and flesh and the mercy of the goddess that he is capable of traveling and returning back with the memory of what he learned while he went there. It is through Freyia's drink of precious mead that he may remember what he learned. In the Hyndluljóð, there is a deal of bickering between Freyia and Hyndla, where it is made clear that Hyndla, despite all her knowledge, offers only death and oblivion when it comes down to all things. Freyia, on the other hand, who identifies herself as Hyndla's sister, is the one who offers memory and resurrection from death, and who is willing to take Óttarr all the way to Valhalla, a state of eternal resurrection – which is what immortality means in Old Norse myths.

This pairing of two female character representing death versus life, oblivion versus memory, keeps repeating itself in Norse myths. In the myth about Iðunn, we also have two female characters who represent two opposites; Iðunn is what makes the gods renew their youth and resurrect eternally, while Skaði, whose name actually means injury or harm, and she forces the gods to give her justice and atonement lest she destroy the gods. Skaði, like Hyndla, lives in a realm crammed with wolves, winds and mountains, a realm of death in many ways.

The Realm of Death: Wolf

We see that an act of sacrifice has led to a journey into a realm of giants and of death – another world, dangerous and mortal, where important treasure has been hid – a very common theme in Norse mythology.

But is it the realm of death that we are speaking of?

Yes, after a fashion. In the second stanza of Haustlǫng, we heard that Iðunn is an eloquent, wise woman, and that Thiazi, the slave-binder, is her "wolf" – as in that which hunts her. In this, Iðunn is akin to Sól, the Sun goddess, who is constantly hunted by another wolf. The Moon and Óðinn are also hunted by a wolf, so this is not just a female theme.

The Sun gives us her rays of light, Iðunn offers immortality, Óðinn offers spirit, and the mysterious Moon god has a mighty power and represents the counting of time – and they are all hunted by wolves – or rather THE wolf, the one who stays bound only until Ragnarǫk, known by names such as Fenrir and Garmr and Hate-Witness – all associated to qualities that are the very opposite of what they are hunting; rage, greed, hate, fear.

The wolf and the dog are animals generally associated to the realm of death, often associated with dangerous giantesses, although as we have seen, an Iron Age goddess much worshiped, Nehalennia, was once also portrayed with a dog or a wolf on her right-hand side – while there is a basket of apples in her lap and to her left.

The Eagle of Death

In the same second stanza, we learn that this wolf-like abductor of the wise woman created a LOT of noise when he flew, and that this noise comes from the wind he makes as he is beating his wings. This wind, which creates sound and comes from the beating of eagle wings, is also called arnsug, as in Eagle Suction, and is a direct metaphor for death.

I did go through this earlier, and identified Thiazi, the jǫtunn in eagle hide, with other wing-flapping giants in eagle hide types, all associated with wind and death or mortality, such as Hræsvelgr, the Corpse Swallower, who is mentioned in the Vafþrúðnismál and said to be the origin of the subtle winds that we cannot see, but which permeate all the worlds, and which symbolize mortality and death.

Norse skaldic poetry was all about the art of describing one single thing in endless variation, and we can only understand who or what we are talking about by looking to context, attributes, motifs and functions. Seen this way, it is not hard to understand who this slave-binder really represents. Thiazi is identical to the eagle who sits in the top of the world tree, and identical with the eagle who swallows the dead. He is the ultimate slave-binder, death itself, or perhaps it is better to name him Mortality.

The winds become poetical metaphors for death or mortality, and the falcon or hawk who diminishes the winds and flies out from between the eyes of the death-eagle, represents immortality. While wind symbolizes death and mortality in Norse poetry, wind-shielded or breezeless means the opposite; immortality. In the myth where Óðinn hangs in the world tree for nine nights, it is said that the tree is wind-swept, and the tree is a metaphor for the universe, which is defined by mortality and death.

When Óðinn looks down and picks up the runes, he also gets the sacred drink of poetry and the powerful galdr-songs that he can use to conquer death and gain a seat among gods. In Norse myths, we have places like Hlésey, the wind-protected island, here live Aegir and his nine daughters, and in another Edda poem we hear that the valkyriur live there.

In one poem, Freyr learns that he must endure nine insufferable nights before he can reach the breezeless grove of Barri, immortality. I suspect that the nine insufferable nights belong to the same category as the nine nights that Óðinn sent hanging in the tree before he got all these divine gifts, or the nine nights it takes to reach the heart of Hel. In other words; the myth of Iðunn has many layers, but ultimately, the theme is death and immortality.

It is said that the eagle sits to the northern end of the world, in the top of the world tree. North is, in Norse mythology, always the direction of death. The expression north and down still exists in modern Norwegian when cursing someone to death – you curse them north and down. We still use this expression in modern Norwegian; "nord og ned". In Old Norse, it was norðr ok niðr.

Níflheimr

Basically, the realm of death lies in the north, and from there on its only downhill. It is in the north that Hel lies, and before it became Hel, it was called Níflheimr, the Misty World. It is one of the three realms that existed before the universe came into being, even before the gods. Snorri told us that there were three parts of the early pre-cosmos; the southern end was full of fire and poisonous gases, and this was called Muspellheimr.

Then there was a northern end full of ice and mist and darkness, and this was called Níflheimr. In between lied a realm in which there was nothing at all, the Ginnunga Gap. Gap means an open mouth, indicating a mouth that opens to swallow something. Ginnunga sounds to me like a combination of the words ginnr, which means sacred, and unga, which is the genitive plural of ungr, which means child or descendant. So I translate Ginnunga gap as the open mouth of the sacred descendants. Apparently, this was a non-place where nothing existed.

Streams of heat from the southern reached the empty mouth, as did streams of cold from the north, and voila, a huge giant was born, Ymir, whose name indicates the sound of a voice. He was nourished by a great cow, Auðhumbla, who brought heat from the south. Auðhumbla nourished herself on the cold world of Níflheimr, and as she licked at the ice of Níflheimr, the misty world, the ice melted, and another giant emerged, Buri, who became grandfather to the gods. His name could mean Storage Chamber.

It could seem that this Storage Chamber giant had been lying there within the icy death of a previous world, re-emerging to life by the actions of the great cosmic cow. It basically means that the origin of the Aesir gods lies within Níflheimr, the world of the dead, the same that is now called Hel of Níflhel, ruled by the lady of the dead. Later on, Níflheimr became the world of the dead, lying to the north of the universe, which is also the direction of the giant in eagle hide and his world Þrýmheimr, the Drumming World.

So we have to do with a giant in eagle hide who is a poetical metaphor for mortality and death, and this, my friends, is the antagonist of our story, Death, no less. I also mentioned Veðrfǫlnir, the falcon or hawk that sits in between the eagle's eyes, like a third eye or something, and who is able to diminish the winds of the eagle, that is, able to diminish the power of mortality. Incidentally, Loki wins when he assumes the hide of the hawk or falcon, a hide that is referred to as Freyia's Válshamr.

As said before, the val is a heiti for hawk or falcon, but is also the word used for those who have fallen because they have been chosen to go to Valhalla, which is in fact a state of eternal resurrection from death. The blot leads to a journey into the northern realm of death, and Iðunn also ends up there as a consequence. As a consequence for Iðunn ending up in the realm of the giants who rule the spheres of high mortality, the gods become old and grey and dying.

Loki must travel there in order to restore the goddess, and put on himself the val-hide, the cape of immortality, owned by the goddess Freyia. With this cloak, he saves Iðunn from the giants and from death, but is hunted by death all the way until he reaches the world of the gods - and immortality through eternal resurrection. When Iðunn is brought back, the gods become young again and are healed.

Shamanism

Travels to the worlds of the giants and the worlds of the dead – worlds that often seem to overlap with each other in the way they are described – are extremely common in Norse mythology. I would go as far as saying that such journeys form a central theme of the Edda myths. We already talked about how Óttarr had to sacrifice to the goddesses in order to invoke Freyia, so that he may take the shape of the dying boar and enter into the underworld with the guidance of the goddess. While in the underworld, he learns about sacred wisdom, about how all the lineages in the world are related to each other, and come together in one singular, original character, Heimdallr.

Or when Óðinn sacrificed himself on the wind-swept tree, looks down into the worlds at the roots of the tree, sees the runes of fate that the norns had carved into the world tree, and painstakingly brings them back up to the world of men, alongside what he learned of spell-songs and the mead of poetry that he took from Gunnlǫð within a mountain – a typical place for the dead.

These are just a few among many similar stories that appear to be mystical journeys of initiation, perhaps akin to the initiation stories of classical mystery cults, but also clearly related to the phenomenon we tend to call shamanism. Shamanism is an umbrella term. The word originates among the Tungus of Siberia, where the sáman is the tribe's intermediate with the spirit world.

The sáman may either call on spirits for help, or else travel out of body into various spirit realms, including the worlds of the dead. In this culture, mortal illness is often explained as the soul of the person being lost or held captive in another world. Healing someone from sickness usually means that the sáman makes a ritual in which he or she travels into the other worlds in order to seek out, free and bring that soul back to the world of the living, the world of human beings.

It is very common to imagine that one is traveling out of body while borrowing the body of a beast, such as a bird, a snake, a typical steed animal or any other animal. In order to reach a state of perception that allows for such a spirit journey, music, dance and not the least, a steady, hypnotic, rhythmic beat, like that of a drum or a staff, is applied. This basic concept is something we find in many different cultures all over the world, what testifies to its antiquity.

For the last century or so, the umbrella term shamanism has been used for this phenomenon regardless of culture or language. As you may have noticed already, some sort of shamanism seems evident in the Haustlǫng myth; and the shaman of the story is of course, Loki, who must travel into the other world in order to retrieve a being whose existence is vital to the health and lives of the gods. The story involves references to rhythmic beat or drumming, as well as a staff, and there is reason to believe that they thought that a sacrifice may provide the steed needed to ride down into the underworld.

SAVING THE SOUL OF THE GODS

Let us take another peak at Óðinn sacrificing himself to his own self on that wind-swept tree. He looks down into the worlds that lie to the roots of the universal tree. The norns, goddesses of fate, have carved the runes of destiny into the roots of the tree. Óðinn sees them, grasps them, and screaming, he brings them up, brings the mighty runes of fate into what is said to be the shrine of Earth – Iarðar Vé.

Along with the runes, he gets a drink of the sacred mead of poetry from a giantess seated on a golden throne, who here goes by the name of Gunnlǫð, and with whom he swears a ring-oath, and he is gifted with nine powerful galdr-songs. The result, as it says in the Edda poem Hávamál, is that he gets a place among the gods, and becomes a great sage. Yes, this is exactly what is said; when he brings these treasures up to the world of gods and men, he gets his seat among the gods. This is what makes of him a god.

What does it mean, that he comes among the gods as a result of this death journey? It means that he reaches a state of immortality, in the form of eternal resurrection – and since we know that Iðunn is the source of this state of immortality, we know that this divine state is given by the grace of the goddess. So this is relevant to the Iðunn story; it is exactly immortality in the form of eternal resurrection that the goddess Iðunn offers, just as Gunnlǫð offered this to Óðinn when she gave him a drink of the precious mead from her golden seat.

It is likely that the sacrificial animals were regarded as some sort of steed into the other world. When gods and men in Norse mythology are about to travel into other worlds, they either ride an animal – usually a horse or a boar, or they apply the hide of an animal. If the animal has just died, like in an act of blot, that is, an act of sacrifice, it is very likely that it had the quality needed to bring someone down into the underworld, because the animal was on its way there already, so that the blótsmaðr – the sacrificing man, could, in some way or other, tag along. In the Haustlǫng, we see that Loki joins the dead ox on its way to the realm of the dead, exactly as Óttarr joins the dead boar.

Loki is glued to the staff he applies when he wants to beat the eagle, and the staff is glued to the eagle carrying the dead ox. We do know that people who practiced seiðr, used staffs. I should add that whereas everybody probably knows that Siberian shamans often used a drum to travel with, it is less known that using a staff to make the beat and to travel with was also common in Siberian shamanism, especially among women shamans. We know, from countless tales of shamanic practice, that both physical and psychological illness and death was often regarded as a result of having lost one's soul. The soul was considered capable of wandering away without you, and the soul could be captured or get lost.

Many shamanic journeys are all about the shaman traveling down to the underworld in order to find and free the lost soul. In this myth, we hear that Loki must travel to Þrymheimr, that is, to the drumming world, in order to find Iðunn, and we know that drumming beats are vital to shamanic ecstasy and other-world-journeys. In other words, we have to do with a form of Norse shamanism where the journey to the underworld is all about saving a goddess who seems to, poetically, at least, refer to the soul of the gods itself, the force of life, knowledge and renewal, and resurrection from death.

I actually think that this myth is about blót and the shamanic aspects of seiðr, and about what the blot really did for people – that through the sacrifice, one could establish a channel of connection to other worlds and open a sort of portal for venturing into other worlds, such as the realm of the dead. This could also be a part of some sort of mystery initiation where it was possible to reach a state of immortality or a promise of immortal existence after death, but one would have to go through a sort of ritual death state in order to reach it.

The story of Iðunn's abduction fits perfectly into the typical story of shamanic soul-retrieval, in which Iðunn plays the role of the soul that is lost. When the soul is lost, it has to be retrieved, lest the ones who own the soul grow sick or old and die. The soul is rescued through a shamanic feat of traveling outside of the body and entering the world in which the soul has been captured or lost, rescue it and bring it back. Then the owners of the soul retrieve their health alongside their soul. But does this mean that Iðunn actually represents the soul of the gods? Well, like any other mythical character, Iðunn may have poetically represented many different things in different contexts, but I would go as far as to say that in this particular poem, in this particular myth, Iðunn does represent the soul of the gods, their immortality.

WHAT DOES THE NAME IÐUNN MEAN?

- **iða (f.):** an eddy, that is, a water stream which turns from the main stream and directs itself back towards the watersource, creating a whirlpool effect.

- **ið** (f.): action, deed

- **ið-** (pref.) : returning, towards

- **iðinn** (a.): eager, determined ivrig

- **iði:** splendour, shine, awesomeness/ (a): hard work

- **Iðuliga (a):** repeated, renewing, continuous

- **Iðavöllr:** The fields where the streams turn back towards the source, where the surviving gods shall gather after Ragnarök, and where the world itself is renewed and ressurected.

- **Brunnakr Bekkjar Dís:** Goddess of the Benches of the Water-Source-Field

WHAT DOES THE NAME IÐUNN MEAN?

In order to explore the possibility that Iðunn represents the one soul of the many gods in this particular narrative, we must take a look at how the goddess Iðunn is described in skaldic poetry, and what her name means. We have already talked about how gods and goddesses may take many names, and that the name chosen is usually relevant to the particular context of a story, indicating what that character is meant to signify in that story.

The meaning of her name is probably derived from the noun iða (f.): an eddy, that is, a water stream which turns and directs itself back towards its origin. When the water stream turns, it is met with the main stream of the water flow, and a spiral whirlpool effect happens, which is the eddy; the Ida. It could possibly also come from another noun, ið (f.): Which means an action, a deed, a work, or else from the related word ið- (pref.) : Which means returning, or towards, or it could come to the adjective iðinn (a.): Which means eager, or else shiny and magnificent, or else from the adjective Iðuliga: which means repeated, continual, renewing.

Her name is also connected to the place name Iðavellir: the fields where the streams turn back towards their source, where the gods shall gather again after Ragnarök, in order to renew the world. If we think that Iðunn in this myth actually represents the immortal soul of the gods, the one who gives them life and eternal renewal, then her name itself suggests that she is the one who creates action, who puts things in motion, the one who drives to seek back to their origin so that they may be renewed and conquer death.

I usually prefer the more specific eddy-meaning of her name, partly because it just makes sense to me, and also because I think this meaning is indicated in the kenning used for her where she is the goddess of the benches of the water-source field, the brunnakr bekkjar dis. She represents that movement – back to the origin, back to start, for a new revival. The theme of streams is ongoing in Norse mythology.

The norns who live by the well of origin in the heart of Ásgarðr to the south of the world, where the gods and goddesses meet up for parliament to rule the world together, well, these norns keep watering the world tree with water from the well of origin, the Urðarbrunnr. This water has the quality, Snorri explains in the Gylfaginning, that if you go into it, you will come back up completely new, transparent and shining.

Another quality of this water is that it renews and rejuvenates the universe tree, and serves to counter the constant decay that the tree is also experiencing. Another water-source lies to the east, and this is where the giant Mimir, whose name means Memory, drinks of the well of memory. In this well lies all the memories and knowledge that has been stored from every world in the universal tree. This is where Óðinn left his one eye, so that he could drink from it and become omniscient like the universal memory giant himself.

A third water-source lies to the north, in Hel or Níflheimr, and this is the Resounding Mill, in which the souls of the dead are gathered, and from this well come all the rivers of the world. All the rivers. So, let us have this straight; the souls of the dead come into this well, and out of this well flow the rivers that go through all the world.

Obviously, the rivers symbolize something else than rivers. It sounds to me that we may as likely be speaking of souls. If you think that the world of the dead is a strange place for souls to originate, recall how important it is to go into that world in order to achieve immortality, and recall that the gods themselves emerged out of the misty ice of Níflheimr, the world of the dead that existed even before this universe came into being.

In one Edda poem, Vafþrúðnismál, three rivers of the universe, streaming out of the resounding mill water source in Hel, are said to be hamingjur, female spirits who bring fortune or in some way or another are associated with fate. The term hamingja only means luck in modern Icelandic, but back in the days, it seems that the hamingja was a form of norn or fylgja, a female spirit being who follows individuals through their lives and affect their fates as they go.

These following spirits could either be divine, elfin or dwarfish. It was said that every individual got a fylgja or several fylgjur at the time of birth, and that these would follow the individual all their lives and spin their fates. The term hamingja appears to indicate older functions, as it could mean "one who walks in a hide", that is, something non-physical that appears in a physical hide. In other words, it appears that Iðunn's name has to do with streams and what these symbolize, not the least when they return to the water-source, to their origins. And it has to do with action, renewal, repetition, and also with something that is magnificent and shiny. I would personally call that force - the soul.

Kenningar for Iðunn

In the skaldic poem Haustlǫng, Iðunn is referred to as an eloquent, knowledgeable and wise woman. If we consider the possibility that she represents the immortal soul of the gods, then the soul is what promotes wisdom and eloquence. She is also known as the maiden who knows the age-cure of the gods, in the sense of being the one who can cure them of old age and thus allow them to become young again, over and over and over.

She is the goddess of the benches of the water-source field, the Iðavǫllr where the gods shall gather again when the world has ended and the new world is to begin. That she is the goddess of the benches of this field means that she has power over who gets to sit there. This reminds me of how Freya is said to rule the benches of her hall, Fólkvangr, which means people field, a place where Freya receives the vál and chooses who gets to stay with her and who must fight on in Valhalla. This is where Freyia rules over the fate of the souls after death.

When Freya rules the benches, it means that she has power over who gets to sit where in the after-life. Iðunn is also the precious maiden who increases the joy of the gods. And she is the beer-Gefn, the beer-provider. The heiti Gefn suggests a connection to Freyia – again, since Gefn is a typical Freyiuheiti, but when that is said, the name is also used for the giantess Skaði and for the vǫlva Gróa in the same Haustlǫng poem.

Skaði is the Gefn, the provider of the mountains, and in a stanza we did not go through because it belongs to the other half of the poem where another myth is told, the vǫlva Gróa is called a beer-Gefn when she heals Thor. From the heiti Gefn, the name Gefion appeared a separate goddess, one who sees all fate. The beer insinuates the sacred drink which gives knowledge and helps the drinker to escape the realm of death and even remember what happened while there.

Then we have the kenning Ása Leika – the lover of the gods. As in, the one, singular lover of all the gods. This is very interesting; she is actually the lover of all the gods here. She is not named as the wife of a single god, but rather as the one who belongs to all of them. She is what they have in common, their single marker, what they all share; and she is what makes them into gods by offering eternal resurrection. There is only one other source which mentions a goddess who is the lover of all the gods, and that is from the Edda poem Lokasenna, where Loki reveals that Freyia has been the lover of every god and every elf in the hall of Aegir. Which means that she was everyone's lover. But what does that mean?

We think about sex, immediately, what with Freyia and all, but the hall of Aegir is situated in a place called Hlésey – the Wind-Shielded Island. As I have explained before, wind is a metaphor for death, while wind-shield is a metaphor for immortality. This means that Freyia has been the lover of every immortal soul who have gathered here in this place of immortality.

Freyia is a receiver of the dead, and it is a fact of Norse skaldskáp that death was always referred to in sexual terms; to climb into bed with Freya, Rán, or Hel, in whatever guise or by whatever name she applied in that story, was the same as dying. So whenever there is a sexual scene in a skaldic poem, we should think of death. And so, when Iðunn is referred to as the lover of the gods, it may mean the same as what it means when Freya is said to be the lover of gods and elves in the hall of the immortals; their love is an embrace of death, when the soul is united, perhaps, with its origin, or taken back to its origin by the grace of the goddess of eternal resurrection.

Iðunn in the Raven Galdr

In another poem that we shall discuss in part 3, Iðunn appears with year other kenningar. I shall only relate the ones in stanza 6 for now, since these kenningar also appear in a new light if we think of Iðunn as the immortal soul of the gods.

It reads;
Dvelr i Daulom
Dís forvítin,
Yggdrasils frá,
aski hnikin,
Iðunni heto
Áfa ættar,
Ivalds ellri,
yngsta barni.

There dwells in the valleys
a knowledge hungry goddess
The Seed of Yggdrasill
sinks down the ash
Her name is Iðunn
of Elf-Kind
Of the oldest of Ivalldi's;
the youngest child

The poem says that Iðunn dwells in the valleys, that she is a goddess who seeks knowledge, and that she sinks down the world tree, back towards its roots. It says she is the seed of Yggdrasill, the seed of the world tree – the key to its resurrection. Yes, I did name my book after this. She is of elf-kind, which is significant, since elves and the souls of the dead are frequently mixed up in the sources, and dead people may be referred to as elves.

There are two kinds of elves, the dǫkkálfar, the ones who live in the darkness of the mounds and make precious metal things, quite overlapping with the dwarfs, and ljósalfar, the light elves, who dwell in the upper heavens, the ones where Hel does not rule, and where death cannot reach. One of these worlds is called Víðbláinn – which means wide death. The other immortal light elf world is called Andlangr, which means long breath or long spirit. So when it says that Iðunn is of elf-kind, we do get some associations to death, the afterlife and the theme of immortality.

It also says that she is the youngest child of the oldest of Ivalldi's. Ivalldi may be translated as the in-ruler, that is, the ruler within. So she is the youngest child of the within-ruler's eldest. It is all subtle, but it all points to the soul, at least that is how I see it. All in all; these kennings from the Raven charm are similar to the ones in the Haustlǫng in the way they emphasize Iðunn's association to knowledge or the quest for knowledge. She is the seed of the universe itself, both the source and the fruit at the same time. She moves through the universe, and she is of elf-kind, closely connected to concepts of immortality.

She is both the oldest and the youngest, the origin and the new; the two sides of death. When Loki is taken by the Slave-Binder, it is death and mortality that he meets. He trades in his soul to death in order to get free that moment, and has to conquer death by entering the world of the dead in the shape of the one who is chosen for resurrection, and by bringing the immortal soul back into the realm of the gods.

Summing up: She is a knowledge-hungry, eloquent, wise woman, and the theme of mind and consciousness and wisdom is strong in this story. She knows the age-cure of the Aesir, that is, she sits on the secret to immortality. She is associated to the seats of a field of origin, where the new world will emerge after Ragnarǫk. She is both the oldest and the youngest of the ruler within. She is the seed of the universe – both its fruit and its origin.

She is precious, increases divine joy, and she offers the drink of memory, poetry and immortality. The drink she offers is the same sort of drink that Óttarr was given by Freyia so that he may remember his universal interconnectedness that he learned while in a state of death. She is of elf-kind, what sets her in connection to the light elves and the sun goddess, the light elves living in the highest heavens and who are immortal.

Hel does not rule here, and the gods eat together with these light elves in Aegir's death-shielded island. She is the lover of all the gods, and this does not mean that she is a slut, it means that, like with Freyia, every god and elf had a loving relationship to her in connection with rejuvenation and resurrection from death. Her apples have the same quality as the water of the well of origin that the norns own; that the one who bathes in it, or who eats these apples, will emerge renewed, shining and transparent. She represents, I think, the universal soul, the spark that gives motion, purpose, direction, inspiration, and the quest for learning.

What is a soul?

In order to determine whether it makes sense to interpret Iðunn's role in the Iðunn-myth to be the role of divine soul, we must look to what the soul is. I guess that most will agree that the soul is the part of us that may possibly live on after the body dies, it is something that is within us, and which may possibly exist outside of us too, especially after we die, and perhaps before we were born. If we believe in reincarnation, we may think of the soul as that part of us which goes through each incarnation. If we do shaman-stuff, we might say that the soul is that part of us which travels into other worlds in a shamanic context, or when we dream.

Even if we do not believe in any form of after-life existence, we may simply see the soul as that part of us which constitutes our core personalities, the spark that drives us towards learning and understanding, the spark that makes us thrive when we do something we feel soulfully passionate about. In the Old Norse language, there were different words that could be translated as soul. Sál is the word that was used when Norse people took to Christianity and needed a concept for the immortal self which would either be saved and go to Heaven, or denounced to Hell after death.

But the word itself is older than that and may either come from older words for life-spark and vitality, or else associated with older words for water, which is really interesting when we think of how Iðunn is associated to water streams and to soulful things like learning and renewing. Another Norse word for soul is the sefi, which is used more frequently when referring to emotional states and feelings, and also for mind or passion. In one Edda poem, a valkyria who plays the role of personal fylgja for a prince is said to come from Sefafjǫll, which means the Mountain of the Souls.

Yet another Norse word that could be used to describe the soul of a person, especially the part that has to do with intent, mindset, will, thought and passion, is the húgr. Óðinn has a raven called Húginn, which sort of means the mind or the thought or the intent or the passion or the mindset; this part of Óðinn can fly like a raven through all the worlds and bring back knowledge. It is the Húgr that is sent out on shamanic travels to other worlds, often taking the shape of an animal, said to be wearing an animal hide. I already mentioned the elves being somehow connected to the souls of the dead.

This does not mean that the elves ARE the souls of the dead, but that their identities and functions overlap and that dead people are sometimes referred to as elves. When we hear of higher heavens where only light elves dwell, and where there is no death, it is not unthinkable that we have to do with a realm of immortal souls, the souls who have conquered death. I also spoke of the hugr as a part of the soul or the self that may move outside of the body. And then there are concepts such as the fylgja and the hamingja; female spirit beings who are closely connected to our individual fates and who appear at birth, like guardian spirits.

The animal fylgja appears to reflect on the individual's personality and status in life, and may appear in dreams where the actions of the animal fylgjur symbolize the fated actions of their individuals. Seeing one's own fylgja while awake was regarded as an omen of death. The female fylgjur seem to be a mix of the souls of ancestral mothers who follow and guide their descendants, and a sort of guardian spirit. The name of Hamingja seems to point to an earlier function were the spirit being represented something that moves inside the physical body. Basically, it is possible that all these beings are in some way or other connected to the human soul or maybe are parts of the human soul.

Comparative Soul Concepts

If we look to comparative mythologies, we quickly find that the concept of an all-soul or a universal soul is quite common. In old Egyptian mythology, we find the concept of the all-soul in many different settings. One is where the goddess Isis represents the all-soul, the universal soul from which every other soul derives. The ancient world abounded with mystery religions where one went through a ritual death initiation in order to unite with the universal soul, represented by the great goddess. She was called the saviour, the goddess who would free the soul from the cycle of life and death and offer salvation through resurrection in a land of immortals.

Similar concepts are found in old Indian mythologies, where the all-soul is represented by a god or a goddess and where the goal of the wise is to achieve union between the individual soul and the great all-soul. Both in India and in the classical world of mystery religions, this spiritual union with the all-soul or the universal soul could be described poetically as a marriage or a sexual union. In Tantra, it is believed that the gods and the goddesses all exist within us, and that each individual is like a copy of the great universe. The goal of tantrism is to make the self reunite with its origin. In Old Norse mythology, the gods and goddesses and other powers also do seem to represent qualities that exist within human beings. Óðinn could represent both spirit and breath, the very source of life within us.

He appears in a trinity where other qualities associated with spirit are also given, such as thought, mind and poetry, and passion, life-spark and color. I do not have time to go through all of that here, but I wrote about this a lot in my book The Seed of Yggdrasill; how the stories and the characters may really be stories about different qualities within us, interacting, uniting, separating, re-uniting, conflicting, aligning – all while trying to reach a state of immortality. The idea that a goddess may represent the universal soul, the one that we must seek to re-unite with, the one that the gods are united with, is an ancient and widespread idea.

I already mentioned classical mystery religions which abounded for thousands of years in the ancient world, some of the oldest ones being found in Egypt. I mentioned tantra and other Old Indian paths of enlightenment involving the idea that the gods are within us and outside us at the same time, and that we must strive towards reunion with the all-uniting universal soul. I could make another lecture about this, so we are just summarizing here.

Old Indian sources tell us of a goddess of learning and intelligence, Dhisana, who could be both one and many at the same time; and each individual representation is a wife to the gods, but each wife is really just an aspect of the one goddess. Dhisana's name is etymologically the same as the Norse word for goddess; dis.

Another comparative goddess is the Old Iranian goddess Daena, who can be one and many at the same time. A great goddess of the soul, Daena is both all-soul and individual soul at the same time; each individual has a Daena, whose appearance reflects on the personality of the individual; yet Daena is also one. When we die, we will meet our Daena, and her appearance will reflect on yourself; if you were a jerk, so to speak, she would come to you at the moment of death like a shrieking, hissing hag, but if you were a nice person, she would come to you at the moment of death like a beautiful maiden. Sounds familiar, does it not?

GÝGR OR MAIDEN — THE FATE OF THE SOUL AFTER DEATH

The Iðunn myth comes with two female characters who appear to be absolute opposites. Iðunn with her apples of immortality and only bright and sweet metaphors to describe her with, versus the giantess Skaði, who demands justice and atonement, and who takes pleasure in harm and in the howling of wolves.

In this story, they appear like two opposites, and this pairing of two females who represent stark contrast, like life versus death, is a repeating theme in Norse mythology; there can be no Maiden with the Mead without the mention of a vicious hag. Only in the character of Hel - the goddess of the dead - do we find the two opposites united in one; her face is half blue like a rotting corpse, and half rosy and bright like a blushing maiden.

Going to Hel – in the sense of dying, is frequently described as making love to her in skaldic poetry. I mentioned before that the Iron Age goddess, Nehallennia, may in the same way represent the two opposites, with a basket of fruit representing knowledge and immortality on one side, and a dog who represents death and oblivion on the other. What character you will meet when you die, or when you visit Hel – and we know this because there are many stories about it, well, if you meet the vicious giantess, there will be only death and oblivion. But if you can keep the giantess at bay until the maiden appears, then you will reach a state of divinity. To end this part 2 of the lecture series about Iðunn, I will sum up the kenningar for two other characters in the story; Thiazi and Loki.

HEITI & KENNINGAR FOR THE EAGLE OF DEATH

Slave-Binder (Thiazi)
Corpse-Swallower (Hræsvelgr)
Very Wise Corpse Swallower (Válkastar)
Ghost of the Giant World
Mountain Howler (wolf)
Wolf (abductor) of the Eloquent Woman
Fortress Beast of the Providing Woman
Partly Un-Blended Treason
Battle-Hungry Ruler of the Wagon of Friendships
Hungry Father of the Giantess
Educator of the Ski-Goddess
Giant Child
Lineage-Tree of Hýmir
Son of the Lover of the Grasping One

HEITI & KENNINGAR FOR LOKI IN THE HAUSTLǪNG

Friend of the Raven-God (Hrafnásar vínr)
Hænir's (Mind's) Friend (Hænis vínr)
Hænir's (Mind's) Intent-Tester (Húgreynandi Hænis)
The Stirrer of the Stories (Sagna Hrærir)
The Wise God (Fróðr Tív)
Child of the Hawk (Öglis Barn)
The Cunning-Clever Defier of the Gods (Bragdviss ásvifrandi ása)
Deep of Soul Hiding God/Beast (Djúphugadr hirdi-Týr)
Heavy Air (thungr Loptr)
Belt-Thief of the Flaming Gods (Brisings goda girdithiófr)
Thor's Confidante (Ófrúni Thors)
Father of the Wolf (Ulfs Fadir)
Son of Fárbauti
The Burden of Sigyn's Arms (Farmr Arma Sigvinjar)

Iðunn Part 3: Hrafnagaldr Óðins eða Forspjallsljóð

Odin's Raven Charm or Song of the First Speech

Introduction to Part 3: Edda Poetry

Hrafnagaldr Oðins eða Forspjallsljóð is an Icelandic poem in the style of the Poetic Edda. The title translates as "Odin's Raven Galdr or the Song of the First Speech" – the first speech meaning a prelude to something else. Perhaps it was meant as a prelude to other Edda poems? In order to understand why this poem hardly ever makes it to any ordinary translation of Edda poetry, we need a quick introduction to our written sources, concentrating on Edda poetry. The Edda poems have come down to us by way of many different manuscripts. The most complete manuscript that survived to our day is a 1270 A.D. copy of an earlier manuscript, known as the Codex Regius, or else as the Sæmundar Edda.

This manuscript was given into the hands of one Brynjolf Sveinsson back in 1643, after having been hidden by a mysterious and unknown family of Icelandic farmers who, for reasons we do not know, had kept it safe for some three centuries - perhaps safe from persecution by medieval church authorities? Incidentally, and quite poetically, the last surviving – and near complete - manuscript surfaced from oblivion only a few years before the temple of Nehalennia also resurfaced in 1647, after being hidden beneath the ocean for a thousand years. By the time Brynjolf received this old book into his hands, these pagan poems were no longer perceived as a threat to the ruling religion, and was rather recognized as a treasure from the past.

In this manuscript, the Edda poems have been placed in a chronological order that make a lot of sense, and it is common for all modern translations to place the poems in the same order. It was believed that the Codex was a copy of an earlier, lost manuscript that had been written down around the year 1100 by one Sæmundr Fróði (Sæmund the Wise) Sígfusson, who lived between 1056–1133. Sæmundr was a priest and a scholar. He was one of the first to write a History of the Norwegian Kings in the Norse language, a work that has been lost to us, but which we know was one of the main written sources to Snorri Sturluson's Ynglinga saga and Heimskringla.

While the poems, in the form we know them, have been dated to the late 10th century, that is, the 900ds, and probably first composed in Norway, they were later written down in Iceland before or around the year 1100. As I have mentioned before, paganism was not outlawed in Iceland until about 1100, so the original book was written during Sæmund's lifetime, probably while many Icelanders were still openly pagan. The book was copied several times, and was obviously known to Snorri back in the 1200ds, since Snorri kept quoting them during the 1220s.

However, even in Snorri's time, restrictions abounded; in his Prose Edda, Snorri completely left out the most deeply pagan parts of the Edda lore; he does not ever mention the initiations of Óðinn or Gullveigr, for example – we only know about these events from Edda poetry. These Edda poem manuscripts and other very early works - written in a time when the tenets of the new religion were still a bit blurry and mixed up with pagan beliefs - may have been persecuted, since we only know them from later references. For centuries, only a few of the poems survived as pieces within other works that quoted from them. The only (near) complete Edda manuscript that survived, our Codex, probably survived because it was hidden away from the authorities by people who – for reasons we do not know - regarded it as precious.

According to Icelandic folklore, Sæmundr began his life as a pagan, and learned the dark arts and made a pact with the Devil so that he was brought safely back to Iceland from Europe on the back of a seal. Fortunately for Sæmund, and less fortunate for the helpful seal, a bible popped up on the beach before him when he reached his home shores, and, having become a Christian, Sæmundr used the holy book to beat the poor and helpful seal to death, thus conquering the Devil.

This folklore about a great scholar who lived during the long centuries of conversion is clearly a blend of pagan and Christian perceptions, mixing shamanic narratives of supernatural, shape-changing and helpful travel with the negative reactions of a Christian audience, perhaps one of the many originally pagan themes that were being re-shaped in order to make their audience forget the purpose of the pagan lore and teach them how to think more like Christians, perpetually condemning the pagan elements of the story as devilish and bad, no matter how life-saving and benevolent that seal-shaped devil had actually been.

Whether Sæmund the Wise was the one who wrote down the Edda poems first or not, we cannot know for certain. Bishop Brynjolf believed it was so, but this notion has later been questioned. Whoever was really behind the first manuscript, we know that it was copied several times, and we have fragments from several different copies in addition to one surviving manuscript, probably copied during the early 13th century, a little before Snorri wrote his other works. We know that the Medieval Church would often persecute books that were deemed dangerous to their tenets, and many of these earliest chroniclers may have had very blurred boundaries between the pagan mindsets of their parents and grandparents and the newer ideas from abroad.

I think it is entirely possible that persecution of books was the reason why so many early books vanished or only survived in fragments or revised copies, and may be a reason why "The Poetic Edda" as a whole manuscript was hidden away by people who had obviously also taken care to preserve and protect it – most likely from Church authorities. Thanks to the efforts of people who saw the need to preserve this part of history even when it was illegal, we have access to a body of mythical, poetical lore that is closer in culture to the original pagan form than most other European works on ancestral lore. In most other places, ancestral lore was usually written down several centuries after the Christian conversion of these countries.

Even if lore kept being orally transmitted, centuries and centuries of Christian perception of what is being told will, inevitably, alter the pagan stories quite radically before they are finally written down, what we may also see in Icelandic sagas of the 14th century in particular: Even when dealing exclusively with the oldest of legends, these late works display a much heavier Christian influence on both events and how the characters of the stories are being perceived by the chroniclers, than what we see in earlier works that were closer in time to the pagan past. While the Edda poems keep dealing with deeply pagan subjects such as sacrifice, death-journeys and initiation, testifying to having been written down earlier when there was still a higher tolerance for these things, it is clear that by the time of Snorri Sturluson, caution was exerted.

Snorri was smart, however, and avoided persecution by claiming that all the pagan stories are valid for as long as we consider the gods to be human ancestors rather than actual gods. He could even point to several ancient, Scandinavian royal dynasties who counted their lineages back to their gods, so this claim to gods being ancestors was not even that far-fetched, but rooted in pagan lore itself. With this careful approach, and this ancestral emphasis, Snorri was able to render most of the stories he knew about without getting persecuted, myths for us to enjoy to this day. We can find almost all the Edda poems in this manuscript, with few exceptions.

A few pages have been torn out of the manuscript, and we can only guess which poems were lost, and whether these are the same as other poems we have found in other manuscripts, or simply completely lost to us. By studying the language forms used in an old text, linguists are able to date such texts with relative accuracy. It is now generally believed that even if we do not find Edda poems written down any earlier than the 11th century, that is, just after Christianity had become a major influence in Scandinavia and Iceland too, poems such as the Vǫluspá and many other Edda poems were in fact composed quite in the form we know it, sometime during the late 10th century, that is, the late 900ds[22], in Norway.

TIMELINES

872: Norway is united beneath the king Haraldr Harfagri/ Harald I Fairhair. Many Norwegian chief families escape his tyranny by moving to Iceland.
Ca.880-900: Haustlöng composed by Thiodolf the Wise
930s: Hákon the Good tries to unsuccessfully convert Norway to Christianity
900-1000: Edda poems are composed in the form we know them
960s: Denmark is officially Christened
1000: The Icelandic Parliament votes for Christianity as a state religion (paganism is still legally practiced)
1030: Norway declares Christianity as a state religion
Ca.1100: Paganism is outlawed in Iceland
Ca.1100: Christianity official religion of Sweden
Ca.1100: Edda poems are written down
Ca.1100: Sæmundr the Wise the first to write books in the Norse language
1178: Snorri Sturluson is born
1220s: Snorri writes Heimskringla & the Prose Edda, preserving a lot of Skaldic poetry
Ca.1400-1600: Hrafnagaldr is recorded (written down-the date of composition is unknown)
1643: The Poetic Edda Manuscript resurfaces

---

22 Sørensen & Steinsland (1999): Voluspå, Pax Forlag, Oslo, kapittel 1

1647: The Temple of Nehalennia resurfaces
1650s: Eirik Hallson tries to decipher the Hafnagalr
1728: The great fire in Copenhagen destroys the oldest paper where the Hrafnagaldr was recorded. The only recording left is a thwarted paper in the Stockholm library
1867: Sophus Bugge declares that the Hrafnagaldr "should forever be left out of the Poetic Edda collections & translations"

The 10th century - this means that we are still in the Viking Age, and that most of the Norwegian and Swedish populations were still pagans, just as some half of the Icelandic population were still pagans when the Edda poems first were written down a hundred years later. It is also likely that many of the Edda poems were composed in the form we now know them in Trøndelag, Norway, during the 900ds and here it is important to note that in Norway, Christianity was not established as a state religion until 1030. In Iceland, Christianity became a state religion already back in the year 1000, but age-old, democratic principles meant that paganism was not outlawed; it would take almost a hundred more years before paganism was outlawed in Iceland.

This means that the 11th century, the century when most of the Edda poems we know were being recorded into written books, was a time when both Christianity and Paganism existed side by side. Since the poems were composed at least a century before they were written down, they were composed in an era that was still ripe with paganism. Trøndelag, where most of them were likely composed, at least the Vǫluspá, was besides a stronghold of paganism; here you found the earls of Hlaðir, who were the last to make a pagan stand against Olaf the Holy back in 1030.

This means that many Edda poems are certainly expressions of pagan people who were by now defending their old religion and their old customs against a new religion. And when I say "composed in the form we know it", it does not mean that the poems were not based on much older myths – many of the myths of the Edda have archaeological and comparative counterparts that are very old, and many point back to actual historical events of the 2nd-to 5th centuries AD.

Hrafnagaldr

However, some of the Edda poems were not written down until much later – and we – or rather, learned linguists, can tell by looking at the language forms, since language and spelling systems changed with time. This does NOT mean that the poems were not composed a lot earlier, neither does it mean that they are not also based on very old lore, it just means that we do not have earlier recordings of them, only later.

Most of the earliest texts from the 11th century have been lost to us, and we have only later copies recorded by hand, centuries after, and the more a manuscript has been copied – by hand – the more we are likely to find some errors or slight changes to the texts. The Raven Galdr represents one of the poems that have only been found in a very late manuscript, although there are signs that there was at least one, far older manuscript that got lost in a fire in Copenhagen back in 1728. Sadly, since this manuscript burned up, we have no way of knowing how old that was, or if the chronicler had left any information about the paper he had copied.

The Lost Poem

As said, The Raven Galdr has come down to us by way of very late papers. We know for certain that it existed by 1650, when we have records of an Icelandic poet who had tried very hard to make any sense of it – without success. Since this poet was studying the paper around 1650, the poem itself is probably a lot older than that. In 1867, the Norwegian scholar Sophus Bugge published a complete overview of our Old Norse written sources, in which he recommended that the Raven Galdr should forever be left out of future translations, since he believed that it was a late fake. In his explanations, he refers to earlier attempts at deciphering the poem, and that most have considered it indecipherable:

> "Guðmundr Magnusson tells us (...) that the Icelandic poet, Erik Hallsson, who lived around 1650, for ten years studied this poem and finally threw it away with the confession that he understood little or nothing thereof..."

Back in 1867, Sophus Bugge, who otherwise did us the great service of re-recording countless old, Norse texts, dismissed the poem as a very late addition, not from the pagan period at all.

"I have earlier expressed the opinion, that Forspjallsljóð is no older than the 17th century; it is though already proven, that it existed already by 1650, and probably earlier than that. Little information may be got from the words; "In a letter from Arni Magnussson to Mr. John Haldorsson, priest of Hitardal, dated June 18th, 1729, about the books he had lost in the great fire of Copenhagen 1728;..."

"Our Rector, the late Ólaf has written to me, about what papers have been burned, regarding one of these poems of the Sæmundar Edda (Poetic Edda), if I remember correctly, Hrafnagaldr Óðins, that Magister Brynjolf have let this poem be recorded after one single, old and dirty paper, which he, as far as I remember, certainly states was defect in the end. This is now for me like in a haze, since I have lost the documents. But the poem may also be found in Cod.Stockh.Isl.Chart 57 fol, where the poem is recorded on its own, this manuscript was probably recorded between 1670 and 1680, and it is already in these manuscripts in many places thwarted, which means that it must have been re-written many times already."

Interestingly, John Haldorsson claimed that the poem belonged to the Sæmundar Edda, which is what they still called the Codex Regius, and it should here be said that a few pages were indeed missing from this manuscript. Haldorsson also suggested that the paper that existed in Copenhagen was old. But due to the great fire in Copenhagen in 1728, the only version that has been left to us is a copy found in the Stockholm royal library – a late version copied by someone who was clearly not very professional, an unlearned student, perhaps, so that it is full of spelling errors, grammatical errors, and is also defect in the end.

Hrafnagaldr Oðins – Authentic or Not?

Prior to 1867, the poem was always a part of translations of the Poetic Edda. But in 1867, Sophus Bugge, who was a great authority in this field, dismissed the poem as a very late addition that had no place in the original texts, and since then, it has rarely made its way into any modern translation, but must be found in separate studies. Why? Sophus Bugge reasoned that the poem should be excluded because it certainly came out of a different standpoint than the other Edda poems. These poems were, according to Bugge, clearly folkloric, all recorded out of the beliefs and concepts and poetical perceptions of the late pagan era, clearly transmitted from mouth to mouth for hundreds of years.

The Raven Galdr, however, was clearly made by someone learned, someone who knew the poems by heart in their original language, someone with a strong understanding of ancient poetry, and who was trying to copy the poetry of old. He states that it was likely composed in written form first, not orally by some Viking Age skald. Besides, Sophus Bugge thought that the poem was so hard to translate, understand and decipher, it was pretentious, artificial. He did not understand the poem, and so it was said by many others – Eirik Hallson had studied this poem hard some time during the 1650s until he confessed that it was not possible to understand it.

For these reasons, Bugge concluded that the complexity of the poem in itself made it stand out as different from the others, and that there were also certain modern, by modern we are speaking of the 17th century, modern Icelandic elements in the language, suggesting that it had been composed in written form no earlier than the year 1600. However, as we have heard, there was an older manuscript, of which the age is not known, that got burned in Copenhagen in 1728. The other, flawed manuscript was the one that existed in Stockholm at the time, and is the only one that we are left with. It is said to be a late copy, obviously copied by some less than bright student (although, thank to this student, we still have a version) - and it was said to be linguistically thwarted and full of spelling errors, and that the ending was missing.

Sadly, we have only been left with this late copy, difficult to decipher and translate because it is full of spelling errors - and the end is missing. This does not necessarily mean that the poem is quite as late-composed as Bugge claimed. Back in 2002, Jonas Kristjánson argued that the poem was probably as old as the 14th century, that is, the 1300ds, which means that the poem could be dating from the time of the Bubonic Plague. The age of the poem as we know it is still being argued among the learned, so we must conclude that nobody really knows for certain exactly how old the earliest manuscript may have been, nor how old the myth of the poem, or the original poem, was.

And, say, it was indeed just composed at a later stage. It is still an interesting poem, and the author clearly knew almost, perhaps even as much, about mythology and poetry as any skald of old. Paganism took centuries to truly vanish from the perceptions of people. It was in 1220 that Snorri Sturluson noted that young people of his era – young people back in the early 13th century, had begun to no longer understand the poetry of their ancestors, because they no longer took the mythical worldview that these poems were based on, for granted.

Iceland chose Christianity for their state religion back in the year 1000 AD, and it was literally a 50-50 vote. This means that when Christianity became Iceland's state religion, 50 % of the population was still pagan. Half the population, still pagan. And because they had very old, democratic principles, paganism was still allowed for almost another century. When the first manuscripts were written down by Icelandic monks and scholars, half the population was still pagan.

When Snorri stated his sources, he points back to old people who remembered the lore of their pagan parents. At some point, the Catholic Church became more strict. Paganism was outlawed before the year 1100, but texts about pagan lore were still permitted. However, we see a clear difference between the older, Poetic Edda works, and Snorri's Prose Edda explanation of these works: he is an amazing storyteller who clearly knew his subject, all credits to him, but by 1220, more than two centuries after the conversion, young people were losing the older worldview, and Snorri had to omit several crucial scenes that we only know from the Poetic Edda.

•Óðin's hanging? Poetic Edda. You will not find a word of it
in Snorri – except through clever allusions, such as when he
tales the tale of Gunnlǫð and the mead of poetry.
•Gullveig's burning? Not a word in the Prose version,
although he helps us along by explaining how Freyia traveled
the world and was a vǫlva, the very first teacher of seiðr.

Around this time, the stories of how Óðinn and the goddess
conquered death and achieved resurrection – a form of salvation
through seiðr, galdr and sacrifice- and how this helped them
reach a divine state, were no longer acceptable to describe openly.
Incidentally, this time of censorship is about when the complete
Edda manuscript I was talking about, was hidden away. Hidden
away, so as to protect it from Church prosecution. Hidden away
by people who cared. It is not at all unthinkable that some pagan
traditions were secretly preserved, especially among the learned,
and by those who were studying old poetry.

I think that the Raven Galdr, in the form we have received it,
may be echoing a late pagan surviving tradition, and even if not,
it is interesting to see what some learned poet of the late medieval
period, someone who was clearly well wandered in the language
and pagan lore of his ancestors, and also clearly passionate about
it - tried to tell us in the riddle language that is Old Norse poetry.
I shall be the first to admit that yes, the poem is extremely hard to
translate, not the least because it is full of spelling errors, so much
so that translators sometimes have to guess. I tried to translate
it once, back when I was studying the Old Norse language, and it
was truly incomprehensible for a newbie, although I got something
sublimely interesting and mysterious out of it – even if it may not
have been correct.

The only stanza that really made sense to me already back then was the one about Iðunn. It was from this stanza that I got the inspiration for the title The Seed of Yggdrasill, from Yggdrasills Frá, a kenning for Iðunn. The rest was compelling and fascinating, but not understandable. The translation I shall present to you in this lecture is sort of my own, but in this version, I have relied heavily on other and more experienced translators of the text, such as Eysteinn Björnsson and William P Reeve's 1998 translation, Anette Lassen's translation from 2011, and Benjamin Thorpe's 19th century translation. By comparing these with my own understanding, I have come up with a translation that may vary a bit from others, but still within the acceptable norm – and rest assured that all the other translations I have come across do vary a lot from each other also.

I have made my best to find compromises and make sure that it is not directly wrong, even if many a sentence is still open for discussion. I have tried to render it in a form that makes as much sense as it can, being a very cryptic poem. When working with this sort of hard-to-translate and hard-to-understand text, you sort of have to determine a main understanding of the poem and then see if the translation really fits. My main understanding of the poem come from when I first held a lecture about Iðunn for a bunch of modern Heathens at Idavollen in Norway three years ago. After my lecture, they held a blót in honor of Iðunn, and then performed a sort of play-act of the Raven Galdr where it was clear that Iðunn was the main, female character.

This was also argued by Victor Rydberg in 1866, one of the few scholars who disagreed with Sophus Bugge's claim that it was non-authentic; Rydberg also claimed that it was about the theft of Iðunn. Now, Rydberg may have been wrong about things, but the idea that the poem is about Iðunn does make a lot of sense, and he has not been the only one to see the theme of the loss of Iðunn as the main theme of the poem. I shall now go through the poem stanza by stanza, and we shall try to see if it makes sense to us if we place Iðunn in the place of the main female character. Iðunn is only named once, and otherwise referred to in kenningar and heiti. As I have explained before, this was the common way of describing a character.

It was also perfectly common to replace the name of a goddesses with the name or heiti of another goddess – we would know the true identity from the context, or else start to realize that divine identities were indeed as fluid and overlapping as they seem in pagan poetry. For the poem clearly also indicate other story lines known from the Eddas, and sort of unite them into one single story.

I want to remind you all that the key to Norse poetry is to say one single thing in countless different ways, just as we can describe one single goddess in countless different ways and apply to her countless different names, even borrowed from other goddesses, and that the choice of name or heiti or kenning in each situation is a conscious choice intended to point to a subtle meaning, a riddle that has to be solved.

For this reason, it makes perfect sense to let different stories come together and overlap with each other, since they may all just be different poetical expressions of the same core theme: the eternal quest for the resurrecting goddess in the underworld, the one who needs to be restored above.

The divine soul, perhaps.

STANZA 1: INTRODUCING THE POWERS

1.Alföþr orkar,	1.All-Father is able
álfar skilia,	Elves discern
vanir vitu,	Vanir know
vísa nornir,	and Norns will show (the
elr íviþia,	way)
aldir bera,	The Witch Within Wood*
þreyia þursar,	nurtures
þrá valkyrior.	The Ages bear
	Thurses endure
	Valkyrias yearn

The first line; Allfaðir orka, is of course a reference to Óðinn as the All-Father. The verb orka means to be able to do something. Anette Lassen (2011) translates this as "exerts power", while Björnsson & Reeves translates it as "works". But – what is he able to? How does he work? Or exert power? Over what? What this is referring to is obscure, like so many things in this poem. It should be said that all Edda and Skaldic poetry would have been equally cryptic and obscure if we had lacked prose explanations such as those provided by Snorri Sturluson.

What makes this poem particularly difficult (apart from the spelling errors that open up for many different possible interpretations) is the seeming lack of context, the lack of prose explanations. Norse poetry was all about alluding subtly to a story that they expected the audience to know already. Our biggest problem when interpreting this one is the fact that we are an audience who are not familiar with the story that the poet is alluding to with metaphors and hints.

The second line; Álfar skilia, is a reference to the elves. The elves, apparently, are able to skilia – "to separate", as in to understand, or to discern. Again, we have no explanation as to what they understand.

The third line; Vanir vitu, is pretty straightforward; the Vanir know. What they know in this case, and what the elves understand, and what Óðinn is able to, is not explained, although the Vanir are frequently referred to as wise and knowing. It was among them that the most powerful of all crafts, seiðr, emerged. Freyia, the goddess of the Vanir (Vanadís), taught that art away to the Aesir (Ynglinga saga 4).

In the fourth line, we learn that the norns, the goddesses of fate, they will show us – but what? The way? Our destiny? We do not know. We do know that the norns set the laws of the universe and decided on all fate, and that they are responsible for keeping the universe "tree" alive.

The fifth line, elr iviðja, introduces what I call "the witch within wood". Iviðja literally translates as "in(side) wood", but from other contexts, we know that the iviðja also refers to a giantess or even a sorceress, such as a vǫlva. Giantesses and vǫlur frequently overlap, such as the giantess Gróa ["To Grow"], who is also a vǫlva and a healer, or the giantess Gríðr ["Truce"], who has the son Víðarr with Óðinn, and who lends out her wand, the Gríðarvǫlr ["The Wand of Truce"] to Thor – the very term vǫlva derives from the vǫlr, which refers to her staff of office. In the Edda poem Vǫluspá, stanza 2, the oldest of vǫlur declares that she remembers nine worlds and nine witches within wood before creation:

2.Ek man jötna ár um borna, þá er forðum mik fœdda höfðu; níu man ek heima, níu íviði, mjötvið mœran fyr mold neðan.	2.I remember giants born before time They who in the olden days had me fostered Nine worlds I remember, nine witches within wood (Before) the precious Measur- ing Tree (=Yggdrasill) grew from the ground below

The vǫlva who tells the story of our world in the Edda poem Vǫluspá mentions nine iviði in connection with nine previous worlds – as in previous "world trees" (i.e., "wood) – before she and the new world tree rise from the ground. I think that the reference to being inside wood is important, as the wood is a poetical metaphor both for the universe (the universal "tree") and also for the human body, and there appears to be a concept of a primordial giantess-vǫlva in connection with the "wood" that symbolizes the physical universe. This is why I translate it as "witch within wood".

The verb elr, Lassen translates as "strives", while Björnsson
& Reeves (B&R) translate it to "gives birth", and Thorpe writes
"brings forth". I have not found this word in my dictionaries, but as
the poem had spelling errors in its only surviving edition, it could
certainly be, as B&R and Thorpe have suggested, meant to be elur,
and this may indeed mean "gives birth" or "brings forth". It could
also mean "raises" or "brings up", "feeds", "nurtures" or "harbors"
(you could use the word to say "harbors resentment," "nurtures
hatred", or any other feeling one may nurture.

It could also specifically just mean "nurtures-", "gives birth to-"
or "raises a child", and so I finally settled for "nurtures", since
"gives birth" seems too specific when the word is used in so many
ways, while "nurtures" can mean all these things; referring to
something you carry inside, something you also produce or help
grow. But what is it that she nurtures? Most scholars seem to think
that this must, of course, be the mysterious giantess of Jarnviðr
– "Iron Forest" – who brings forth the monsters that will swallow
the world. I have tended to think that her nurturing has more to do
with the ages that are mentioned in the next line; aldir bera – "the
ages bear (endure/carry/bring forth)"

Aldir may mean "the ages", and could of course refer to the ages
of men. In modern Icelandic, it appears to be a common way of
saying "centuries". Going back into Old Norse-speaking ages,
we know that there existed concepts of different ages in history,
and Óðinn is actually referred to as Aldafaðir – "Father of the
Ages" more often than he is referred to as Allfaðir – "All-father".
However, the "ages" could also be a way of referring to human
beings throughout history, hence both Lassen, Björnsson and
Thorpe have translated this as "humans bear" or "men endure".

Again, to me, this sounds too specific and limiting, because aldir
refers to humans throughout the ages, not just to "humans". To
simply write "men" or "humans" is a translation that loses the
historical emphasis of the word, that this is something that humans
bear or endure throughout the ages of history. The verb bera may
in some way be used to mean almost the same as elur; it can mean
"to carry", but also "to endure" or even "to be pregnant" or "to
give birth". It can have the more specific meaning of delivering
something. This means that aldir is doing much the same thing
as the iviðja; they are striving to "bear" something – or perhaps
"bear" something forth. The ages of history and the iviðja – the
witch within word - are doing the same thing, enduring, carrying,
bringing forth.

This does make sense in the context of how the iviði exist at the beginning of time, connected to the nine previous universes, and perhaps giving birth to the tenth; our universe. The Heimdalargaldr declares that Heimdallr, whose name literally translates as the Awesome World, was born of nine giantess mothers, so it makes sense to think of the nine iviði as those who strive to bring forth – the ages. The two last lines refer to thurses and valkyriur. A thurse, or þurs, is the same as a jǫtunn – a giant, but is usually applied in connection with dark magic and to particularly dangerous giants. Hrímþursar – frost thurses – are among the foremost enemies of Thor, since they often hurl frosty rocks against Earth, his mother, and Thor's primary duty is to protect Earth, Miðgarðr and Ásgarðr. These hostile beings are now waiting. Waiting something out, in an enduring sort of way.

The valkyriur, on the other hand, are yearning for something. Something they desire, as is indicated by the word þrá. What are they yearning for? What is it that valkyriur want? In popular imagery, valkyriur serve ale in Valhalla and bring the chosen slain to Valhalla. But in Edda poetry, valkyriur act as guardian spirits to men who have managed to win their love through great virtue and the overcoming of obstacles. For as long as a man is not worthy, the valkyria waits and yearns while sleeping her life away in a troll-sleep, a spell-induced sleep, until her chosen man finds a way to wake her up, like Sígurðr Fafnisbani does in the Edda poem Sígrdrífumál.

Similarly to his predecessors, Helgi Hiǫrvarðsson and Helgi Hundingsbani, he meets his valkyria – in fact wakes her up from her troll-sleep - only after overcoming mysterious obstacles which enables him to carry the "Red Gold" up a sacred mountain. There, he discovers a valkyria sleeping, her armor having grown into her body, cuts her loose and wakes her up. The valkyria immediately proceeds to teach him everything about the runes of fate, how to heal and achieve much the same powers as Óðinn did after his initiation by hanging on the World Tree.

STANZA 2: THE MEAD OF POETRY

2-Ætlun æsir	2. The Aesir could guess
illa gátu,	a difficult purpose
verpir villtu	they threw warping (confu-
vættar rúnom;	sion)
Óþhrærir skyldi	against the spirits' runes
Urþr geyma,	The Mead of Poetry
máttk at veria	is for Urðr* to guard
mestum þorra.	- Not in power to protect it
	from the mighty winter

This stanza is tricky. Lassen has translated the two first lines, which together make a sentence; ætlun æsir illa gátu, as "The Aesir divined the whole plan", while B&R prefer "The Aesir suspected an evil scheme". Thorpe writes: "The forebodings the Aesir suspected to be evil".

•Ætlun is a feminine noun meaning "plan", "intention" or "purpose".

•Æsir (Aesir) means "gods". In this sentence, the gods are the acting parts, while ætlun is the objective, that which is acted upon.

•The adjective illa could mean anything from "bad", "evil", "difficult" and "painful" to "wicked". It looks like it applies to the word gátu, but since gátu must be the verb of the sentence, illa should rather be applied as an adjective to ætlun.

In Norse poetry, the grammatical cases meant that words could be placed anywhere in a sentence, and one would understand where it belonged in the sentence not by where it is placed, but by the grammatical case. You may have noticed this when we went through the Haustlǫng before; The words of the stanza would be placed according to rhyme (also letter-rhyme), rather than according to where we moderns might think it belongs in the sentence. If this had been a modern sentence, it would probably have read; Æesir gátu illa ætlun: "The Aesir could (see) the bad intentions (evil schemes)".

When B&R use the verb "suspect", they must have paid heed to the expression: ill gáta, which means a "suspicion", but which literally translates as a "bad guess". Here, ill is the adjective to gáta, which means "a guess", "a riddle". For some reason, B&T have chosen to use the adjective illr on two words in the sentence; resulting in "The Aesir suspected an evil scheme". If this was correct, we should have a sentence reading; Aesir illa gátu illr ætlun. Since the adjective can only refer to one of the objects in the sentence, we must choose. Is it Aesir gátu illa ætlun – The Aesir guessed/could (solve) the bad intention/purpose? Or Aesir ætlun illa gátu – "The Aesir intended (to solve) the difficult riddle"? Both possibilities must allow for some grammatical errors in the original, flawed text.

This is the other problem with the Hrafnagaldr – our only sample, the only paper that survived the onslaughts of time, appears to be full of grammatical and spelling errors, and sometimes we must guess our way to what is really meant and be open to the possibility that a word could have been written down in the wrong grammatical form. But it could just as easily be; "The Aesir suspected a plan" or "The Aesir could (solve/see/overcome/make) a difficult/wicked/bad/painful plan/intention/purpose." I ended up with a compromise, of sorts; "The Aesir could guess a difficult purpose".

Verpir villtu vættir rúnom is the next sentence in this stanza.

- •Vættir should be the substantive noun of the sentence, and could be translated to "spirits". B&T have chosen "wights", which probably gives a similar meaning. There were Landvættir "land spirits" and other vættir, the word could also be applied to all sorts of supernatural beings, including the gods, which is why I choose the more general term; "spirits". When the vǫlva in Eirik the Red's saga goes into trance, she lets her audience know that many vættir have come to her after they had sung a song called Varðlokur – "calling the guardians", and that they could tell her about the fate of the land and the people.
- •Villtu may have two meanings. It is either a way of saying "will you", as in "do you want?" or "are you going to?" or it may be an adjective meaning "wild", "unpredictable". This may refer to the vættir, or else to the runes.
- •Verpir may be meant as the verb of the sentence, and then means "throw" or "hurl", as in something the wild spirits do.

•Rúnom appears to be the runes that the wild spirits hurl out, or perhaps rather hurl towards. Runes do not necessarily refer to "letters", they could also refer to secrets or symbols or to fate itself – the runes of fate were originally carved into the world tree by the norns, before they were discovered and mastered by Óðinn.

The first time I tried to translate this sentence, I went for "You want to throw heaviness to the runes". But now, after checking with many other translators, I would perhaps rather translate this as "The wild spirits throw the runes", which possibly could be referring to the casting of lots, as in throwing runes as lots in order to see fate. However, the form of the word for runes indicates that the runes are not necessarily thrown, but rather that something is thrown towards or against them, as in "The wild spirits hurl (something against) the runes".

Lassen and R&B and Thorpe have chosen meanings indicating that the "wights" (spirits) have muddled or confounded something – the runes, even the weather! For all my dictionaries, I could not figure out how their interpretations made sense, but when looking through the explanations of other translations, it became apparent that the reason is, again, the problem with errors in the only source text we have. Verpir, according to R&B, simply makes no sense, especially not in the form it takes, and so we must basically guess what the original text was saying, which evidently opens up for different interpretations.

Since all the other translators have decided that the spirits were causing confusion to the runes (or to the weather), I have opened up for the possibility that what they throw is warping – something that may confound the runes. Fortunately, the next sentence is far easier and more straightforward: Óðrerir skyldi Urðr geyma: "Urðr is duty-bound to guard Óðrerir". Actually, due to the flawed grammar, it could just as easily be said that "Óðrerir is duty-bound to guard Urðr", which is probably how Lassen has seen it when she translates; "The Mead of Poetry had to look after Urðr (Fate)".

However, Lassen's suggestion makes little sense in a mythical context, where the precious mead is always guarded by a female being. Óðrerir, of course, is the mead of poetry, the name meaning "Poetry Stir", as in the drink that contains Óðr – poetry, inspiration, knowledge – everything that Óðinn embodies. It is also referred to as the mead of memory, the ancient mead, or the precious mead. In all myths about this mead, it is guarded by a female; Gunnlǫð, Gerðr, Freyia, Sígrdrífa, Hel and, here, Urðr.

Urðr is the oldest Norn, a goddess of fate, whose name means Origin. She lives by the Urðarbrunnr, Origin's Well, where she waters and nourishes the World Tree with water from the sacred well – and anyone who bathes in that well will come out totally renewed and transparent. By this well, the gods gather to keep parliament. Since Iðunn is likely the real female protagonist in this poem, this ought to be one of the many cases where the name of one female power may be used to describe another one; so here, Iðunn plays the role of the Maiden with the Mead, and is associated with the origin of all destiny. The last sentence is; máttk at veria mestum þorra. Most translators seem to agree that máttk must be an erroneous way of writing máttr – as in "mighty" or "powerful", and most agree that it is Urðr (Iðunn) who is in possession of this power.

The Vǫluspá makes it clear that the three maidens who rule fate are the most powerful of all beings, setting the laws of the universe that even the gods must follow. It is by Urð's well that the gods gather for parliament – the parliament that rules the world. Lassen has interpreted the –k ending as a negative; that there was no power (as in Óðrerir had no power to protect Urðr). It is hard to say what is right, except I am convinced that it is Urðr (Iðunn) who is the protector here. Urðr (Iðunn) either has the power to, or fails to have the power, at veria, "to protect" the mead of poetry from mestum þorra – "the greatest winter." This is likely a reference to a fimbulvetr – "a great winter" that is to come. This again is a reference to an earlier Ragnarök when the winter lasted for years and the sun could not be seen – an actual, historical disaster event following a volcanic catastrophe in 536 AD, a traumatic catastrophe that people expected would happen again.

STANZA 3: THE SOUL SOARS

3. Hverfr því hugr hinna leitar, grunar guma grand, ef dvelr; þótti er Þráins þunga draumr, Dáins dulo draumr þótti.	3. Thus the Soul soars looking for the Other The powers fear harm if he (The Soul) is delayed he thought that the Desiring's dream was heavy He thought that the Dying's dream was illusion/denial

My three primary translation sources of this stanza are widely different from each other, so I will render all of them here:

THORPE (1865):
Hug then goes forth,
explores the heavens,
the powers fear
disaster from delay.
'Twas Thrain's belief
that the dream was ominous;
Dain's thought that
the dream was dark.

LASSEN (2011):
Therefore, his courage fails
He looks for the others
The people (dwarfs)
suspect harm if he delays
Thráinn's thought is
(filled with) a weighty dream
Dainn's thought
(with) a deceitful dream

BJÖRNSSON/REEVES (1998):
Hugur then disappeared
seeking through the heavens
Men's ruin is suspected
if he is delayed
Thráinns thought
is an oppressive dream
Dáinn's dream
was then thought enigmatic

Before we continue, let me make a few things clear; the reference to *Húgr may be a reference to Húginn, the raven of Óðinn, which is usually thought to represent "thought". However, while húgr may indeed mean "thought", it is "thought" in the form of "intention", and it can also refer to personal passion, what one truly wants, and is frequently also used to refer to the soul or even to love.

When translating it to "thought", it becomes too limited, because thought can mean any sort of mind-activity, while the húgr has a lot more to do with a person's soul, intent and passion, and the thoughts that are associated with this. Since the húgr is also the part of the self that may travel outside of the body, I have chosen to translate it as "The Soul". Like Lassen, I am certain that the word hinna refers to "the Other", and when the soaring Húgr is searching for "the Other", I think it could be a reference to Húginn's companion, Múninn, whose name means "The Memory" (or "the one who remembers").

The theme of the danger of oblivion when traveling outside of one's body is ripe in Old Norse myths; Óðinn warns against it in the Hávamál, that even if he fears for Húginn, he fears even more for Múninn, that he – Memory – will not return after having traveled. There are other verses in that poem too, when the god speaks of the danger of forgetfulness. In the Hyndlulióð, Óttarr is in danger of forgetting everything he learns while in the underworld unless the goddess offers him Minnis Aul – the Drink of Memory. Disaster strikes when Sígurðr Fafnisbani forgets his union with his valkyria on the Sacred Mountain in the Sígurðr-poems of the Edda.

It is not without reason that the powers fear harm if the Soul is delayed: As we saw in the previous parts of this lecture, the soul could get lost in other lands, leading to sickness, ageing and death. This is, incidentally, exactly the main theme of the Iðunn-myth. Thráinn and Dáinn are typical dwarf-names, but they also mean something; Thráinn literally translates as "The Desiring One", while Dáinn literally translates as "The Dying One" or "The Dead One".

The Desiring has a heavy dream, while the Dying/Dead has a dula draumr – a dream of illusion; the word dul (f.) Means "hidden", but also "illusion", "self-trickery", "delusion" and also "hubris", as in thinking too highly of oneself. The related verb dula means to deny or refuse, perhaps as in "denial". It could also be, as I have suggested in my translation, that the Soul perceives that the power of desire to be heavy, while the power of death is thought to be an illusion, something hidden, a denial, or something to be refused.

STANZA 4: FALLING DOWN

4.Dugir meþ dvergum dvína, heimar niþr á Ginnungs niþi sauckva; opt Alsviþr ofan fellir, opt of föllnum aptr safnar.	4. The dwarves' ability dwin- dle worlds are sinking down to the darkness of the Sacred Descendant (Gin- nung's) Alsvíðr* often fell from above Often, from the falls, he misses them afterwards

Again, the poem in the form we know it opens for different interpretations:

THORPE (1865):
Among the dwarfs
virtue decays;
worlds sink down
to Ginnung's abyss.
Oft will Asvid
strike them down,
oft the fallen
again collect.

LASSEN (2011):
That's enough of the dwarves
Worlds dwindle away
They sink down to
the darkness of Ginnung
Alsvídur (Odin) often
fell from above
and often gathers up
the fallen again

BJÖRNSSON/REEVES (1998):
The dwarves' powers dwindle
The worlds sink down
towards Ginnung's Abyss
Often Alsvidur
fell from above
Often he gathers up
the fallen again

This stanza is in many ways similar to the theme of the Vǫluspá tale of Ragnarǫk, where we hear about the demise of the dwarves and all the other powers. Here, it appears that the worlds will "sink down" back into the origin of the universe itself; the Ginnunga Gap.

The importance of the dwarves' power must be understood here. In the Vǫluspá, the dwarves are created and named after Óðinn, Víli and Vé ("the sons of Bór") have given order to the universe, but before there is life on Earth, or at least before there was any human life here.

The gods are happily playing around in their newly forged cosmos when three "almighty" and "very powerful" maidens arrive from the world of giants. Their arrival forces the gods to gather for the very first parliament in order to create the dwarves. The names of all the dwarves are listed throughout several stanzas in a poem that only offers small hints to all the greatest historical events since before the dawn of time. Only when the dwarves have been created are the Aesir able to "come through the forms" of the dwarves and enter the Earth (st.17), where they give spirit, thought, mind and life-force to the driftwood that is to become Askr and Embla, the first man and woman.

The word dvergr is translated as "dwarf", but the etymology of the word points to something that is "mutilated" or "limited". It is as if the infinite gods, the spiritual powers, are only able to enter the physical world through the finite forms of "dwarves", and so the "dwarves" are completely vital to the genesis of life on Earth. When their abilities dwindle, as it is said in this poem, I suggest it has something to do with their ability to "hold" the physical world together. Only through their limited forms may the limitless spiritual beings, such as gods, exist within the physical realm.

Now this ability is dwindling, with the result that the worlds
are moving back towards their origin, where they will vanish
into nothingness. Alsvíðr (Very Quick/All-Bright) is a name that
appears in the Grímnismál st.37, where it is the name of one of
the two horses who pull the chariot of the Sun goddess, and in the
Hávamál st.143; after Óðinn has succeeded in bringing the runes
back up to the shrine of Earth and learned how to grow and become
wise:

    142.Rvnar mvnt þv finna
oc raðna stafi,
mioc stóra stafi,
mioc stinna stafi,
er fáþi Fimbvlþvlr
oc gorðo Ginnregin
oc reist Hroptr ra⁄gna.

        142. Runes you shall find
        and runes deciphered
        Very great runes
        Very potent runes
        That the Great Reciter (Óðinn) painted
        And the holy rulers made
        Carved by the Shattered One among the gods

143.Oþinn meþ asom
enn fyr alfom Dainn,
Dvalinn oc dvergom fyr,
Alsvidr iotnom fyr,
ec reist sialfr svmar.

        143. Óðinn with the Aesir
        Dying with the elves
        and Sleeper to the dwarfs
        All-Bright for the giants
        I myself carved some (runes)

In these stanzas, it could appear that Alsvíðr is a heiti for Óðinn
while appearing among giants as a master of runes. It is not
the only place where Óðinn is listed with many different names
according to what realm he appears in or what world; this is
basically the main theme of the Grímnismál, which explains how
the god appears with countless different names according to where
he is and what he does.

The Edda poem Allvismál shows us that every mythical being has a different name according to what "world" they appear in and what function they have there. Óðinn, who is the source of spirit, breath, mind and thought, obviously exists in all realms where his gifts are used; among elves, dwarves and giants. He plays a different role in each.

Why would Óðinn appear among giants? Well, in the Hávamál, it is pretty clear that he learns all his magic exactly from giants. A giantess offers him the precious mead of poetry. A giant teaches him nine powerful galdrar (spell-songs), and a giant gives him a drink of the Well of Memory in exchange for an eye.

The giants constantly appear as teachers and mentors as well as spiritual/intellectual challengers to the god Óðinn, who does not squirm at moving into a world ruled by others than his own. In this stanza, we hear that Alsvíðr, as in Óðinn, particularly when he comes among the giants, often falls, and that he often safnar those who have fallen.

The verb safna is equal to samna, which means to gather, but in the sense of calling a gathering, as in he calls those who have fallen to gather around himself. But what does it mean when we speak of the fallen? It looks to me that the other translators have decided that this is the god collecting "the fallen" as in those who have fallen on the battle-field. These are usually referred to as vál, though, and they are usually collected by the valkyriur. I am convinced that this is, rather, a direct reference to Óðin's own falling from above in the line before.

This, in turn, is probably a direct reference to how he peered "down" before he screamingly brought back the runes as he hung in the world tree – he "fell" - as in falling down into the underworld, where he is endowed with esoteric but powerful knowledge and skill. This is also something he often does, as the Spirit is not just one being, but the spirit in all beings, at least in humankind. And when he gathers to himself those who have fallen, we are not speaking of men who died in battle, but people who did exactly the same as the god; people who also let themselves "fall" down into the underworld in order to achieve said esoteric knowledge.

STANZA 5: STREAMS OF POISON AND STREAMS OF WISDOM

<table>
<tr><td>

5.Stendr æva
Strind né Rauþull,
lopti meþ lævi
linnir ei straumi;
mærum dylsc
í Mímis brunni
vissa vera;
vitid enn eþa hvat?

</td><td>

5.They may never stand firm
Earth nor Splendour (Sun)
Poisonous air
does not cease to flow
neither do the streams (cease to
flow)
that hide in the Well of Memory
- great wisdom

</td></tr>
</table>

Do you understand yet?

This stanza is a direct reference to the apocalyptic Ragnarǫk theme in the Vǫluspá – even the refrain; "do you understand yet, or what" is repeated there. We learn that neither Earth nor Sun are firmly secured, and that there are ceaseless streams of poisonous air to come. Yet at the same time, great wisdom is hidden in the Well of Memory, and streams from there are just as ceaseless.

The Well of Memory contains all the knowledge of all the worlds, and one of Óðin's eyes lie in this well. After a fashion, we are told that nothing is eternal, everything changeable, and that we are (or the world is) being influenced by "flows" of both poison and wisdom in equal measure.

STANZA 6: THE KNOWLEDGE-HUNGRY GODDESS "SINKS"

<table>
<tr><td>

6.Dvelr í daulom
Dís Forvitin,
Yggdrasils Frá
Aski hnigin;
álfa ættar
Iþunni héto,
Ívallds ellri
ýngsta barna.

</td><td>

6. There dwells in the valleys
a knowledge-hungry goddess
The Seed of Yggdrasill
sinks down the Ash;
of elf-kind,
her name is Iðunn;
To the Oldest of the Inner
Ruler's
-the Youngest Child

</td></tr>
</table>

This is the stanza we have discussed earlier, the stanza where Iðunn is directly mentioned and named; she is also referred to in kenningar such as the Knowledge-Hungry Goddess and The Seed of Yggdrasill, said to be of Elfin lineage. This is also where the goddess "sinks" down the Ash. I would not at all be surprised if this was the same sort of "sinking" that Óðinn experienced when he "fell" – after all they are sinking/falling down from the same "tree", the universal tree, a poetical metaphor for the universe itself and all its worlds (the worlds were also sinking, as we saw in stanza 4).

This could be a way of saying that Iðunn descends into the underworld, which is in fact what Iðunn does in the main myth about her; she descends from her place among the gods into the world of death and giants. However, "sinking" also appears in other poems, where "sinking" may mean the same as to be vanquished. In the Edda poem called Helreið Brynhildar, the valkyria Brynhild travels down to Hel in order to save her beloved Sígurðr. Sígurðr is dead, and on his way to the dark oblivion of Hel. Brynhild takes her own life in order to go after and save him, and encounters "the bride of the rock", a giantess who seems to be an aspect of Hel herself.

The Hel-giantess challenges Brynhild by reminding her of all her transgressions while she lived in the world of men, but Brynhild defends herself until she has successfully countered the accusations, upon which she declares that the giantess may now "sink", and that while others must go on with suffering and dying, she and Sígurðr may rest in eternal peace together. The giantess of Death has been vanquished and immortality achieved, and thus, the giantess "sinks" when she loses her power. This too makes sense in connection with Iðunn, whose power is lost to her, or rather, to the gods who depend on her, when she descends into the underworld.

The last two lines go; Ivallds ellri yngsta barna, which literally would translate: Ivalldi's elders, youngest child, which is generally thought to mean that Iðunn is the youngest among Ivalldi's eldest children. The meaning of Ivalldi's name is disputed, but it could literally translate as In-ruler, as in, I suggest, "the Ruler Within", again emphasizing Iðunn's role as Soul, something that exists within, a part of what rules us, the youngest aspect of something very ancient, in the same way that she is a "seed" of the universe – both its origin and its fruit, the key to the next version. In mythology, Ivalldi is the name of the father of the dwarfs who built the ship Skíðblaðnir, made Síf's golden hair and Óðin's spear, Gungnir, great and magically endowed gifts to the gods.

STANZA 7: THE IMPRISONED GODDESS

7.Eirdi illa ofankomo, Hárbaþms undir halldin meiþi; kunni sízt at kundar Nörva, vön at væri vistom heima.	7. It was for little good - her fall from above - to beneath the High Tree held to the tree-trunk; She loathed staying with Narfi's kindred, She was accustomed to better lodgings at home.

This stanza is pretty straightforward, for once. Iðunn's fall is a bad thing, and now she is imprisoned beneath the universe tree, or to the lower parts of the "trunk". She was not at all happy about it, especially since the fall was so great; she had it much better when she stayed among the gods. From this stanza onwards, the Hrafnagaldr provides a theme that the other sources fail to offer; how Iðunn herself actually feels about what happens to her.

Stanza 8: Wedding the Wolf- Hide

8.Siá sigtívar Syrgia Naunno Viggiar at veom, vargsbelg seldo; let í færaz, lyndi breytti, lek at lævísi, litom skipti.	8.The Victory gods saw the grieving Nanna (=woman =Iðunn) They wed a wolf-hide to the Horse's Shrine (Iðunn) She let herself fare with it (she put on the wolf hide) Changed her nature, delighted in/played with illusion, shifted her shape

The Victory Gods is simply a typical reference to the Aesir. The goddess has fallen, and is gone from their world, and now they see her as a grieving Nanna. Nanna is the name of the wife of Balder, who died from sheer grief when Balder died, and then joined her husband in Hel. But the name Nanna/Nönna was also a common poetical way of saying "woman". As we learned in the previous lectures, a goddess could be known by referring to another goddess, and we do know that this "Nanna" is Iðunn, grieving over her loss.

It is my impression that a heiti always means something according to the context, so when Iðunn is called Nanna, it is an indication that she grieved just like Nanna grieved when the love of her life was murdered, so much so that she went into Hel to join him there. Balder represents something important; his abode, Breidablik, means "Broad View", and Balder is indeed open-minded and fair to the extreme. According to Snorri (Gylfaginning), Balder is the wisest among the Aesir, the one who speaks most mildly, and the most compromising, seeing all sides of every case, so much so that his legal judgements cannot work – he is simply too fair, always seeing the best in everyone, and able to see everyone's perspective. In his abode, there can be nothing bad or impure, as it is said in the Edda poem Grímnismál, st. 12:

12.Breiðablik ero in siavndo, enn þar Baldr hefir ser vm gerva sali; a þvi landi er ec liggia veit fǫsta feícnstafi.	12.Broad View is the seventh (world) and there, Balder has raised his halls in that land lies, I know, the fewest harmful runes

Balder is murdered by his brother, Hǫðr Blindi, whose name and nickname literally translate as "Strife the Blind", as in blind aggression. Strife the Blind is led by Loki, who is overcome by his jealousy towards Balder, when he applies Strife the Blind in order to shoot his arrow against the god of fairness and open-mindedness. This is, of course, an allegory; how all that is good, fair, just and accepting of everyone, may be destroyed by the blind aggression which follows from intense jealousy. When Nanna grieves the loss of her husband, this is what she is really grieving; the loss of goodness in the world. And when Iðunn grieves like Nanna grieves, it is likely that she too is grieving over such a loss.

The story of the death of Balder is followed by a charge by his mother, Frigg, who represents love (her name means "Beloved"). She asks who has the courage to travel into Hel in order to ask the lady of the dead to let Balder return to life. Hermóðr answered the charge of the goddess and rides into Hel in order to bring Balder back to life, but the lady Hel refuses. But Nanna sends him back to the world of the living with a gift, a finger-ring to the goddess Fulla, whose name means "the Fulfilled One". Will Iðunn do the same for those who are about to visit her? Or has she changed too much while staying in the underworld?

Now comes the obscure part. We do not know who "they" are, but a "wolf-hide" is given to Iðunn while she dwells in the underworld. The hide is "wed to the shrine", upon which Iðunn, who appears to be the shrine's recipient of the wolf-skin offering, dons the wolf hide, changes her nature, shifts her shape and takes pleasure in – or plays with - illusion, trickery and guile.

This is the only version of the Iðunn myth that we have where we actually get to hear something about how Iðunn herself experienced her abduction or her "fall". She suffers, and the traumatic event leads to a dramatic change in her very nature. A wolf hide – that is, a fierce transformation, and possibly problematic, at least to the gods. She is no longer that sweet, harmonious maiden whose gift is one of renewal and resurrection. She is now like a wolf, dangerous, hunting - a bit like Skaði, actually, the one who mysteriously turns up after Iðunn's return, standing up for herself, demanding justice and compensation, and who enjoy the howling of wolves in the snow-clad mountains.

Stanza 9: Iðunn Becomes an Oracle

<table>
<tr><td>

9. Valdi Viþrir
vaurþ Bifrastar
giallar sunnu
gátt at fretta,
heims hvívetna
hvert er vissi;
Bragi og Loptr
báro kviþo.

</td><td>

9. Víðrir (Óðinn) chose
Bifrǫst's Guardian (Heimdallr)
(ordered him) to ask from
the Carrier/Doorpost of Giǫll's*
Sun
(=the Oracle/Iðunn)
whatever she knew
of the world's affairs
Bragi and Loptr (=Air =Loki)
bore (witness to her) song

</td></tr>
</table>

Víðrir is a common heiti for Óðinn, and means something like "the Weather/Wind-god", in the sense that he is able to control the winds (and thus the weather) with seiðr. As we have seen before, the winds or the weather is also a poetical metaphor for death and mortality. In this stanza, Óðinn charges Heimdallr – the guardian of Bífrǫst, the vibrating rainbow bridge that leads to Ásgarðr – with seeking Iðunn in her new abode below, accompanied by Bragi and Loki. Loki is here called Loptr, "Air", just as he was when he blew the fire of the sacrifice in the Haustlǫng version.

Again, we have three gods venturing together on a journey, but this time they are Heimdallr rather than Óðinn, Bragi, the god of poetry, rather than Hænir, whose gift is the mind, while Loki remains Loki. Óðinn is present as the one who sends the trinity on their way. The purpose of the journey is to seek Iðunn, not as a goddess in distress who needs rescuing, but as an underworld-oracle who may know important things about the world, and who happens to live beneath or in the lower trunk of the world tree.

This is yet another reference to a Vǫluspá theme. In the Vǫluspá, Óðinn seeks the vǫlva and asks her to look into all the worlds. This happens in the middle of the poem, when the world has been created and fate has been set into motion.

We have seen the first war in the world, and how the vǫlva Gullveigr was burnt on the pyre over and over, yet every time, she returns, reborn, stronger than ever:

27. Veit hon Heimdallar
hljóð um fólgit
undir heiðvönum hel-
gum baðmi;
á sér hon ausask aur-
gum forsi
af veði Valföðrs.
Vituð ér enn eða hvat?

27. She knows that Heim-
dall's
listening attention is dis-
guised
beneath the bright, sacred,
radiant tree
She sees a torrent of water
poured
From Val-Father's wager;

Do you understand yet?

28. Ein sat hon úti,
þá er inn aldni kom
yggjungr ása
ok í augu leit.
Hvers fregnið mik?
hví freistið mín?
alt veit ek, Óðinn!
hvar þú auga falt:
í inum mœra
Mímis brunni;
drekkr mjöð Mímir
morgin hverjan af veði
Valföðrs.
Vituð ér enn eða hvat?

28. She sat outside alone
when the Aged One (Óðinn)
came
The old-young of the Aesir
and their eyes met:
"Why do you ask me?
Why do you test me?
I know everything, Óðinn;
where you hid your eye;
in the famous Well of Mem-
ory
Memory drinks the mead
very morning from Val-Fa-
ther's wager."

Do you understand yet?

29. Valði henni Herföðr
hringa ok men,
féspjöll spaklig
ok spáganda;
sá hon vítt ok um vítt
of veröld hverja.

29. For her, the Army-Fa-
ther chose
rings and jewels
For her wise speech
and her magical divination:
She saw widely, so widely
into all the worlds.

This is when the vǫlva actually begins to speak the first verse of the poem, demanding attention from all the world, and starting with her oldest memories, from when she was a young maiden before this universe even came into being. She proceeds by telling everything that has happened until that moment when Óðinn finally seeks her knowledge, and then moves on to predict the future.

This vǫlva, Iðunn, is residing in the underworld, and this theme takes us yet again back to the Balder-myth; In the Edda poem Vegtamskvíða, Óðinn travels into Hel in order to get an explanation as to why Balder had been dreaming bad omen dreams. When he reaches Hel, he rides to the east of the door, the direction of the sunrise, where he wakes up a dead vǫlva by singing válgaldr – spell-songs of the vál – the resurrected dead. She wakes, reluctantly, and immediately reproaches the god, either for waking her up, or for letting her stay dead for so long in the first place:

3...Framm ræið Oðinn, folldvægr dvndi, hann kom at háfv Hæliar ranni.	3. Forth rode Óðinn the Earth-path resounded he came to high Hall of Hel.
4.Þa ræið Oðinn fyrir a/stan dyrr, þar ær hann vissi vǫlv læiði. Nam hann vittvgri valgalldr kveða, vnz na/ðig ræis, nas orð vm kvað:	4. Then rode Óðinn to the east of (Death's) door There he knew of a vǫlva's grave. He sang vál-galdr for the wise woman until she reluctantly rose from the grave and spoke the words of death;
5.„Hvat ær manna þat mer okvnnra, ær mer hæfir a/kit ærfit sinni? var ec snivin sniofi ok slægin rægni ok drifin da/ggv, da/ð var æk længi."	5. "Who is this man, un- known to me he who has forced me to walk this heavy path? I was covered with snow, beaten by rain wetted by dew: I was long dead."

Óðinn hides his true identity and forces her to reply, yet towards the end of this poem, Óðinn discovers that the dead vǫlva has indeed changed. Changed into an ominous being: She answers many of his questions, all the while complaining about having to do this work when she is really dead and just wants to rest, a complaint the god ignores until she suddenly refuses to answer his most important questions.

She accuses him of trickery, of hiding his true self, and he declares that she is no longer a wise woman, but rather the mother of three trolls. This is a reference to either Loki or his giantess lover, Angrbóða; "She Who Bids Rage" – together, they did have three "trolls"; the Fenris-wolf, the Miðgarðr-serpent, and Hel. All three have a role in bringing the world down at Ragnarǫk.

Stanza 10: Preparing for The Long Journey: Seiðr

10.Galdr gólo, gaundom riþo Rögnir ok regin at ranni heimis; hlustar Óþinn Hliþskiálfo í, let braut vera lánga vego.	10. They chanted galdrar (spells) They rode on magic staffs* Rögnir and Reginn (rulers and lords – the three gods) to the edge of the world Óðinn listens from The Opening Vision Shelf* He saw the path was a long journey

I have earlier mentioned the shamanic or seiðr themes of the Iðunn-myth, the presence of a staff, the theme of drumming, and the journey to another world. In this poem, the theme is not only repeated, but elaborated, and is one of the reasons why I think we may take this poem seriously as an Edda poem based on actual mythology and the pagan religion. There is very little here that speaks of 14th-to 17th century (roughly the estimates of when the Hrafnagaldr was composed) cultural practices; rather, it takes us back to pagan rituals.

Here, the three gods travel together to the other world, and they do so by chanting **galdrar – spell-songs**, by **riding on gandr – magical wands or staffs**, and by **meditating in a place** from where one may look into all the worlds: The Hlíðskiǫlf, which means "The Opening Shelf". This place belongs to Óðinn, but other gods may also sit in it. In the Edda poem Skírnismál, the god Freyr borrows the seat and looks into all the worlds, a feat that is followed by a journey into the underworld, where a giantess dwells, offering the Mead of Memory. The journey is long, and we do know this from other descriptions of the path to the underworld.

In the Vegtamskvíða, mentioned recently, Óðinn rode the Hel-path on his eight-legged steed Sleipnir, the one that Loki gave birth to while in the shape of a mare. Óðinn makes the journey in order to seek a dead vǫlva who might know why Balder had bad omen dreams. He rides down to Níflhel ("Misty Hel"), where a Hel-hound, bloodied, barks at him all the way until he reaches the High Hall of Hel.

He avoids the death-hall by riding to the east of it, where he finds the grave of the vǫlva. The east is the direction of the sunrise and must of course symbolize resurrection. Hermóðr, who went into Hel to visit Balder and Nanna, must borrow Sleipnir and ride for nine nights through dark and deep valleys until he arrives at the river Giǫll ("The Resounding One") and rides across the Gjallarbrú – "The Resounding Bridge", and "she (the bridge) is clad with bright gold". Here, he is met by a giantess who asks what he is doing here, he who does not have the appearance of a dead man, and whose presence makes the bridge resound more than it did when it was crossed by five armies of slain men. "Why do you ride the Hel-path?" She asks, and the hero explains his mission before she lets him across, telling him that the Hel-path continues "to the North and down".

In the Skírnismál, Freyr borrows Óðin's vision seat, the Hlíðskjálf, and sees a maiden down in the underworld. His servant, Skírnir, then travels the same path as Óðinn and Hermóðr did before. He must borrow Freyr's horse, the one that can carry him through the dark and flickering flames. It is dark and the path is surrounded by giants as he rides down into the Jǫtunheimar until he comes to the beautiful hall of the maiden. He is met by a herdsman sitting on a burial mound, and the herdsman remarks that Skírnir is neither god, elf, dead or dying, and asks what he is doing there.

The maiden who owns and serves the Mead of Memory, remarks that the hall is vibrating powerfully, indeed resounding, when he arrives, he who is neither dead nor dying, and not even god or elf. For Skírnir is a servant to a god, he is human, and he has undertaken this journey while still alive. This, my friends, is the same path that is now undertaken by Heimdallr, Bragi and Loki as they employ spell-songs and magical wands in order to reach the oracular vǫlva Iðunn in her new abode in the underworld.

STANZA 11: THE THREE GODS ASK THE ORACLE (IÐUNN)

11.Frá enn vitri
veiga selio
banda burþa
ok brauta sinna,
hlýrnis, heliar,
heims ef vissi
ártíþ, æfi,
aldrtila

11.The Wise One (Heimdallr)
asked
of The Drink-Serving Willow
(Iðunn)
-asked about the challenge
of the Bonds (the gods) and their
paths;
If she knew of the origin, dura-
tion
and ageing end -
of the Heavenly Light (Sun/
Heaven)
of the World, and of Hel

In this stanza, the three gods, Heimdallr, Bragi and Loki, sent by Óðinn, have arrived in Hel or the Jǫtunheimar. The two places are frequently overlapping in Norse myths. Iðunn is called the Veigr Selja – the Drink-Willow. The willow is a female tree, and as Snorri explains in his Skaldskaparmál, any female tree can be used as a common poetical metaphor for woman, just as any male tree is a poetical metaphor for man. Such metaphors may also be used for gods and goddesses. In this case, the "willow" refers to Iðunn. The word for willow is selia, which also means "she who sells" or "she who serves (something)", and Snorri explains that the willow is typically employed in poetry to indicate a woman who provides, trades or sells something.

In this context, what with Iðunn now staying in the underworld, this indicates that Iðunn is now assuming the role of the "Maiden with the Mead", the mead-serving woman, just like the goddess Freyia assumes that role in the Hyndluljóð, the giantesses Gerðr in the Skírnismál and Gunnlǫð in the Hávamál and the valkyria Sígrdrífa/Brynhild in the Sígrdrífumál.

Additionally, Iðunn is now endowed with the oracle role of a vǫlva. Like Óðinn asked the dead vǫlva before, so the three gods ask of Iðunn if she may tell them of the future and of Ragnarǫk. And just like the dead vǫlva refused to let Óðinn in on all the secrets, accusing him of letting her stay dead and of hiding his true intentions while expecting her to open up, so Iðunn is no longer the complacent maiden they knew; they have let her fall from grace, and she will no longer help them:

Stanza 12: Iðunn Refuses to Reveal Her Knowledge

12.Ne mun mælti, ne mál knátti gívom greiþa, ne glaum hialdi; tár af týndoz taurgum hiarnar, eliun faldin, endrrióþa.	12.She did not speak her mind nor did she grant any words to the greedy ones She expressed no joy as tears tickled from her skull's shields (eyes) when repressed by pain / bereft of power (her tears) flow red anew

In this stanza, Iðunn refuses to reply to their questions, instead displaying her grief, letting them see her tears, for she is eliun faldin - repressed by pain, or else bereft of power, and her tears are red. It might be a long shot, but this reminds me of how Freyia wept tears of "red gold" over the loss of Óðr – over the loss of her Poetry, Spirit and Ecstasy. This grief caused the goddess to move through all the worlds in her search for her lost passion, taking a new name wherever she came.

STANZA 13: BAD OMENS

13.Eins kemr austan ór Elivágom þorn af acri þurs hrímkalda, hveim drepr dróttir Dáinn allar mæran of Miþgarþ, meþ nátt hver.	13. From the east came, likewise out of the Stormy Waves a thorn from the field of the Frost-Cold Thurse -he who kills rulers - (the thorn) with which Death (Dáinn) visits all (mortals) every night across the precious Midgard

The Élivágar, or Stormy Waves, possibly also meaning the Waves of the Old, are otherwise mentioned by Snorri in the Gylfaginning 3 and 4. This is where the three aspects of Óðinn – The High One, Just-as-High and Third – explain to Gylfi how the world came into being before the gods were born.

There were three parts of this primordial cosmos; the ice cold and misty Níflheimr (Misty World) to the north, the blazing hot Muspellheimr to the south, and the quiet and still Ginnunga Gap, which hosts the origin of the physical universe as soon as the Élivágar begin to run from the well of Hel in Níflheimr, the well called Hvergelmir (The Howling Mill), from where all rivers originate:

“The High One said: `Some rivers are called the Élivágar; when they had come so far from their origins that the poison-cold stream in them hardened – just like the cinder that comes from the melting fire – so they froze to ice; and when this ice ceased to flow, hoar-frost built upon them; and the drizzle rain that stood up from the poison froze into hoar-frost, and one layer of hoar frost laid itself over the other all the way to the Ginnunga Gap.’

Just-As-High said: `The Northern end of the Ginnunga Gap was filled with an enormous amount of ice and hoar-frost that spewed drizzle and odor, but the southern part of Ginnunga Gap cleared up against the cinder that flew out of Muspellheimr.’

The Third said: `But just as cold stood up from Níflheimr (Misty World), and everything there was terrible; so all that was close to Muspell was hot and bright, and Ginnunga Gap was as quiet as the breezeless air. And when the gush of heat met with the hoar-frost so that it melted and started dripping, then life came into these drops of hoar-frost by the power sent by the heat; and it turned into the shape of a man; he is called Ymir (Uttering Sound/Voice) – the hoar-frost thurses call him Aurgelmir (Gravel Howler); and from him are the lineages of hoar-frost giants come…"

Later on, in his Skaldskaparmál, chapter 17, Snorri re-visits the Élivágar and claims that these waves are really just one river which forms the border between Jǫtunheimar, the world of the giants, and Ásgarðr and Miðgarðr, the world of the gods and the world of human beings. The Élivágar are also mentioned in the Edda poem Hymiskvíða, which tells the myth where Thor tries to fish the Miðgarðr-serpent. Here, the giant Hýmir lives at the edge of heaven to the east of the Élivágar, an explanation which in accordance with the idea that then waves, as one river, form a border between gods and giants.

When Thor is often said to be going "east" (east of the river, probably) he is fighting giants. The reference to these waves, or this wavy river, is possibly a reference to how the giants are moving towards hostile attack, and thus a reference to Ragnarǫk, the end of this world which will lead to the start of the new one, just as this world was preceded by at least nine previous worlds. Dáinn is the name of a dwarf, and his name means The Dead One, The Dying One, and may just be a poetical metaphor for mortality or death. This "dwarf" visits everyone in the mortal world of Miðgarðr, a way of saying that death is due to all mortals.

Death applies the "thorn" of the "Frost Cold Thurse" in order to "visit" all mortals; a reference to the law of mortality which we inherited from the first "giant", the physical universe as we know it is a mortal universe, it can and will die, just as we all must. All in all, this stanza reminds us of our own mortality, the mortality of the gods (when without Iðunn), and the mortality of the universe itself. Instead of the wise counsel of the vǫlva, the gods are getting a glimpse of their undoing and a sense of their doom, a reminder of their mortality, just as we learned in the other versions of the Iðunn story; they are doomed to aging and death without the resurrecting power of the goddess.

STANZA 14: MORE ON DEATH

14.Dofna þá dáþir,
detta hendr,
svífr of svimi
sverþ áss hvíta;
rennir örvit
rýgiar glyggvi,
sefa sveiflom
sókn giörvallri.

14.Deeds go quiet, then,
hands slump down.
Senselessness hovers over
the sword of the Bright God
(Heimdallr);
Witlessness a-flowing
into the winds of the giantess
(=the mind/thoughts)
The soul calms, in waves,
the whole congregation

This stanza seems to be a direct continuation of the previous one, elaborating the theme of death and decay. The áss hvíta – the Bright God – is a known kenning for Heimdallr, and I think it is significant that his name means "Great/Noble World". Heimdallr is the god who sees all, hears all, and knows all, the living, conscious, dazzlingly great world, the living, thinking universe itself.

His "sword" may mean his power. Now, senselessness (svímr) hovers over the world, and witlessness (örvítr) are flowing into "the winds of the giantess", which is a common poetical metaphor for thoughts or the mind. The soul is calming down in waves, in the sense of dying little by little, and this happens to "the whole sókn" – the whole congregation – a way of referring to "everyone" – everyone in the world.

Everyone is now doomed - because Iðunn, who rules the resurrection and the renewal of souls, has been lost to us, residing in the underworld. Perhaps this description of a dying experience pertains to the three gods being, after all, in the underworld, experiencing a death which, as we shall see in the next stanzas, do take them to another afterlife realm among the gods.

Stanza 15: To No Avail

<table>
<tr>
<td>

15.Iamt þótti Iórunn
iólnom komin,
sollin sútom,
svars er ei gátu;
sóttu því meir
at syn var fyrir,
mun þó miþr
mælgi dugþi.

</td>
<td>

15. Often, it seemed
to the Yule Beings (the gods)
that Jórunn *(Iðunn)
was swollen with sorrows
when she gave no answer
they grew more persistent
They were faced with her refusal
their many words to no avail

</td>
</tr>
</table>

Stanza 24 continues to emphasize how much the gods tried to persuade Iðunn to reply to their questions, how much they wanted her to be their vǫlva counselor, to reveal the fate of the world, and how useless it was, since the oracle refused to answer. The grief of the goddess is once more mentioned as a reason for why she refuses to reply. In this stanza, the gods are called iólnir, which actually means "The Yule Beings", a common heiti for either "the gods", or more specifically Óðinn, who is also often referred to as Iólnir – the Yule Being.

Yule was a month of ritual celebrations of the gods, and was when the gods were referred to as iólnir. Iðunn, on the other hand, is now called Jórunn. This was a common female name in Viking Age Scandinavia, and the more modernized Jorun is still common, at least in Norway. The –unn ending is a typical way of ending a female name, meaning "woman", although the literal meaning is unnr – as in a small wave, which is employed poetically as a heiti for woman.

Just as diverse words for "goddess" could be poetically applied to human women, so diverse words for "woman" could be poetically applied to goddesses and other female power beings (the same goes for male gods and men). The iór- part of the name refers to a horse or more generally to a steed, something that will bring us somewhere - so we may translate the name as "Horse Woman" or "Steed Wave/Woman/Goddess", a female power who works as a "steed" – something that will carry us on a path, in this setting, especially when the path crosses from one world to another.

In the many Norse myths about journeys from one world into the other, particularly into the world of the giants or the world of the dead, a steed is commonly used for traveling. We have Óðin's "horse", Sleipnir, which may carry the god through and between all the worlds, a horse he lends out to others.

Hermóðr borrows this steed in order to go to Hel and be able to get back again still alive. Skírnir borrows Freyr's steed in order to reach the giant world, Sígurðr Fafnisbani rides his special horse Grani when he reaches the sacred mountain of his valkyria. Freyia uses a boar which contains the soul of a human traveler in the Hyndluljóð, and Loki frequently borrows her falcon hide to use as a steed to the other world. Here, Iðunn is connected to – or may even be - the very "steed" that takes us from one world to the next.

STANZA 16: THE TRINITY TRAVELING AGAIN

16.Fór frumqvauþull fregnar brauta hirþir at Herians horni Giallar; Nálar nepa nam til fylgis, greppr Grímnis grund varþveitti.	16.The First Inquirer travelled the path The Guardian (Heimdallr) of Herjan's (Óðin's) Resounding Horn (Gjallarhorn) The Kinsman of Nál (Loki) he took as his companion and Grimnir's (Óðin's) poet (Bragi) guarded the ground

The different translations I have studied all seem to disagree a little about who is who in this stanza. The First Inquirer may be Óðinn, who sent the trinity on their way, but we know that the path was really traveled by Heimdallr, who works as Óðin's messenger in this poem, so Heimdallr may really be the first inquirer.

This sort of overlapping or unclear difference between Heimdallr and Óðinn is quite common in the myths – they are either two aspects of the same being, or else there were different traditions in which Heimdallr was the great and highest god to some, while Óðinn was to others – it should be noted that which god was the most important and the most high actually varied with time and location – in some places, Freyr was the highest king-god.

There is no doubt that Heimdallr here is behind the kenning "Guardian of the Gjallarhorn", since he keeps the horn and blows it when giants attack. But the Gjallarhorn is also kept by Mímir, who employs it to drink from the Mead of Memory, and Óðinn also drinks through this horn after he sacrificed one of his eyes to the Well of Memory. In this stanza, the Gjallarhorn does not belong to its guardian Heimdallr, but to "Herjan" – "The Lord" – a common heiti for Óðinn.

Whoever really owns the horn that Heimdallr guards, and whoever is really the First Inquirer here, the stanza is clear about Heimdallr taking Loki as his companion, while "The Poet of the Masked One", Bragi, guards the ground. It looks like we are back to start, to before the journey into the underworld in order to ask the oracle Iðunn about the fate of the world, or that this stanza summarizes who went on this journey and what their roles were. Loki, as usual, plays a significant role when it comes to guiding the other gods into the world of the giants, a world that he was born into before he became a god after blending his blood with Óðinn, as is elaborated in the Edda poem Lokasenna.

<u>STANZA 17</u>: THE GODS RETURN TO THE TEMPLE OF THE GODDESSES

17.Vingólf tóko	17. Víðar's* servants arrived
Viþars þegnar	at the House of the Goddesses*
Fornióts sefum	(Vingólf=Friendly House)
fluttir báþir;	The Kinsmen of Fornjótur (the winds)
iþar gánga,	transported them there
æsi kvedia	They walked inside
Yggiar þegar	greeted the Aesir
viþ aulteiti.	at Ygg's (Óðin's) merry ale-feast

In this stanza, the three gods return to Óðinn, who now, interestingly, is keeping a merry banquet in Vingólf – "The House of Friends". According to Gylfaginning chapter 19, Vingólf is a hall situated in the fortress called Ásgarðr, more specifically in Iðavǫllr, and was a hǫrgr – a temple - that belonged to all the goddesses together. It is described as a female counterpart to the parliament of the gods, which was placed in Iðavǫllr, the centre of Ásgarðr, the world of the gods.

Right next to the parliament, there was a temple that belonged to the goddesses, who were no less powerful and no less holy than the gods, according to Snorri:

"First he [Óðinn] set his ruling men [the other gods] in their seats, and asked them to decide the fates of people with him, and rule the running of this fortress [Ásgarðr]. This was in the middle of the gods' fortress, where it is called Iðavǫllr.

The first thing they did was to build a hóf [a temple site] there, where there stood, circling the high seat of the All-Father – twelve other seats which belonged by right to them [the other gods].

This is the largest and best built house on Earth; both outside and within it is covered with gold, and this place people called Gladsheimr [Happy World]. They also built another hall, and that was Hǫrgr [Temple], that the gyðjur [priestesses/goddesses] owned. This was a particularly beautiful house; people call it Vingólf."

Iðavǫllr is also the place from where the new world will emerge after Ragnarǫk, a place of water-springs. As we have discussed earlier, the name Iðavǫllr derives from the same word as the name Iðunn, indicating something that renews itself or returns to the source, like the stream that creates an eddy.

In the Haustlǫng, Iðunn is the goddess of the benches of this water-source-field, which means that she was the ruler of the "seats" here, at least until she fell down the universal tree and ended up in the underworld. It lies at the heart of the world of the gods, holding the parliament of the gods and the temple of the goddesses together. It is also a place where the vál – the chosen dead – are brought, just as they may be brought to Valhalla or to Freyia's Fólkvangr. However, something has happened. Óðinn has taken the high seat in the hall of the goddesses, and is holding a banquet to celebrate there.

This is where the three gods return to after their unsuccessful journey to the oracle Iðunn in the underworld. The three gods are here called by the kenning "servants of Víðarr". Víðarr is the name of Óðin's son by the giantess vǫlva called Gríðr [Truce], and he is said to be a silent god, one of the sons of the gods who is destined to survive Ragnarǫk and help with the creation of a new and just world to come.

When the three gods are said to be his "servants", I believe it means that they are meant to serve this quality; the justice that will prevail after the destruction of the world and help bring about a new and better one. The name Víðarr derives from two words; víð as in "wide" (or rather, "widening", "making wider") and −arr, a common masculine name ending which simply means "warrior".

Víðarr is a god who "widens" something, what makes me think of the name of one of the upper heavens where only "light elves" may dwell, and where death may not reach; Viðbláinn, "Wide Blue One". "Blue" is a common heiti for "Death", so we are speaking of a kind of "wide death", associated with immortality.

The three gods are said to arrive here by the "kinsmen of Fornjótr", a common kenning for "winds" – and winds are heiti for death and mortality. These winds of death have carried the trinity to the immortal heart of the world of the gods, where the chosen dead may go, and more specifically into the temple of the goddesses, where Óðinn has now taken up the rule.

Stanza 18: Hailing Óðinn as the Sovereign

18.Heilan Hángatý,	18. "Whole be you, Hanged God (Óðinn)*
heppnaztan ása,	most fortunate of the Aesir
virt öndvegis	May you preside over
vallda bádo;	the Mead of the High Seat (sovereignty)
sæla at sumbli	Sit, gods, in delight,
sitia día,	at this happy drinking feast
æ með Yggiungi	May you, Yggjungr (Óðinn)
yndi halda.	enjoy eternal bliss."

Stanza 18 reads like a ritual invocation of Óðinn, and may be the words that the three gods apply when greeting their sovereign upon their return to him. Óðinn is called Hangatýr – the Hanged God, a reference to his nine night trial while hanging in the world tree, fasting and stabbed by spears until he picks up the runes of fate, nine powerful spell-songs, and a drink of the precious mead of poetry, wisdom and resurrection from death. He is said to preside over the mead of the High Seat, which may be a way of saying sovereignty. There is also an allusion here to the myth in which Óðinn wrested the mead of poetry from the giant Suttungr by betraying its true guardian, the Maiden with the Mead in the form of Gunnlǫð.

Stanza 19: A New Order

19.Beckiarsett	19. Seated on the benches
at Baulverks ráþi	-at Bǫlverk's* (Óðin's) bidding
siöt Sæhrímni	the tribe of the gods
saddiz rakna;	were sated with Sæhrimnir*
Skaugul at skutlum	Skǫgull* at the table
skaptker Hnikars	meted out the Mead of Memory*
mat af miþi	from Hníkar's (Óðin's)
minnis hornum.	memory drinking horn

Stanza 19 continues to allude to the story where Óðinn steals the mead of poetry from Gunnlǫð, by calling him what Óðinn calls himself in this context, as we may read in the Edda poem Hávamál: Bǫlverkr – "The Harm Worker". It is an admission of having caused great harm.

What sort of harm?

Let us elaborate the story of Óðinn playing the role of Harm-Worker. In the Hávamál, he explains how he sought the daughter of Suttungr ("Heavy with Drink"), Gunnlǫð, and how he actually married her by swearing a ring-oath before he stole the sacred drink of poetry, wisdom and resurrection that she had been set to guard, and left her weeping alone in the underworld:

105.Gvnnlᴀ́d mer vm gaf gvllnom stóli á drycc ins dyra miaþar; ill iþgiold let ec hana eptir hafa sins ins heila hvgar, sins ins svara sęva.	105. Gunnlǫð gave me From her golden throne A drink of the precious mead A bad repayment I let her have after For her whole self For her troubled soul
108.Ifi er mer á, at ec vęra en kominn iotna gorðom or, ef ec Gvnnladar ne nytac, ennar goðo kono, þeirrar er lᴀ́gdomc arm yfir.	108.I doubt that I would have been able to return from the giants' settlements If I had no enjoyed Gunnlǫð That good woman/wife whom I embraced
109. Ens hindra dags gengo hrimþvrsar Hava ráþs at fregna Hava hᴀ́llo í; at Bᴀ́lverci þeir spvrðo, ef hann vęri meþ bᴀ́ndom cominn eþa hefdi hanom Svttvngr of sóit.	109. The next day Frost-thurses came To seek the counsel of the High One In the High Hall Of Harm-Doer they asked If he had met his bane Or if he had been killed by Suttungr
10.Bᴀ́geiþ Oðinn hygg ec at vnnit hafi; hvat scal hans trygðom trva? Svttvng svikinn hann let svmbli fra oc grǫtta Gvnnlᴀ́ðo.	10. A ring-oath, I think That Óðinn swore Who may now believe his word? He betrayed Suttungr when he stole his drink and made Gunnlǫð weep.

In the poem, Óðinn openly admits to betrayal and harm caused, but excuses himself with the result; if he had not done this, the mead of poetry would never have been restored to Iarðar Vé – the Shrine of Earth – forever lost to gods and men, and only for giants to enjoy for as long as it was situated in the underworld. This is the reference we meet in the Hrafnagaldr, when Óðinn is referred to as the Harm Worker – somehow, this is relevant to the story of Iðunn's forced absence from the world of the gods. Where Iðunn used to be the goddess of the beckiar – the benches – of this place, Óðinn has now taken over the ruling of said beckiar.

It is as if a coup has taken place, in which Óðinn, working great harm, had assumed the role of the ruler of who gets to sit in Valhalla or any other equivalent, immortal afterlife. Now, at his bidding, the gods sit there in the hall of the goddesses, and whereas one of the valkyriur, Skǫgull, a female power, is still serving the mead of memory, the drinking horn is now owned by Óðinn, going by his heiti Hníkar – the "Instigator" – the one who instigates something new, such as a new order, a new age. This theme - of Óðinn usurping the power that originally was held by female beings - has its counterparts in other Edda poems.

In the Sígrdrífumál, the valkyria explains why she has been sleeping her life away until the hero is able to wake her up:

2.Hon qvaþ: „Lengi ec svaf, lengi ec sofnoþ var, long ero lyða lę; Oþinn þvi veldr, er ec eigi mattac bregða blvnnstaˊfom.“	2.She said: "Long did I sleep Long was my slumber Long is the suffering of people; Óðinn caused this; that I had no power to change the runes of slumber

Not only is Óðinn guilty of making the valkyria sleep, bereft of power. Her sleep is also connected to the long-term suffering of people. It is when Sígurðr wakes her up that he too may "wake up" - to learn, from her, the esoteric lore of runes, healing and seiðr. The reasons for why Óðinn quenched the power of the valkyria is later explained; the two had different opinions as to who ought to be chosen for Valhalla, and she refused to choose the warriors that he wanted. She had the power to choose the val, and he usurped it, causing her to sleep, and, incidentally, causing great suffering in the world as a result.

This theme repeats itself in several poems of the Edda lore, and curiously seem to take sides with the female victims of Óðinn's bad choices. In the Helreið Brynhildar, the valkyria Sígrdrífa is called Brynhildr, and explains why she had lost her power to choose a worthy man for herself, and why she has acted out of turn, causing suffering in the world when her role as a valkyria should be to cause fortune; it was all due to the greed of "her brother Atli", who is clearly Óðinn in human disguise, and his wish to control who the valkyriur choose.

We even learn that he stole the "hides" of the valkyriur:

6.Let hami vára	6.He stole our hides
hvgfvllr konvngr	The soulful king
átta systra	Eight sisters we were,
vndir eic borit;	born beneath the oak
…	…

This is not the only place where Óðinn plays the villain, stealing power that essentially and originally belongs to female powers. He has been credited with the greatest of all arts, seiðr, yet he learned this art from Freyia, and it was an art considered more fitting for women, even if many men practiced it.

He has been credited with the runes, but the Edda is clear about who really made the runes first; the norns first carved them into the world tree. Óðinn only obtained them, and brought them back up from the trunk and into the world, for gods and men to enjoy. The Flateyjarbók tells a tale where Óðinn and Freyia were married, but then Freyia obtained her Brisinga Mén – her "Jewel of Flames" from four dwarves, and Óðinn charges Loki with stealing it from her. When she discovers the theft, she confronts him in anger and tells him that he has done something bad. He replies that if she can cause an ongoing conflict in the world that will only cease when a mysterious "third" arrives, he will let her have the jewel back.

The reluctant goddess assumes the shape of a giantess called Gǫndul (the Magician), and starts an ongoing conflict between two former friends; metaphorically referred to as the "prince of the Danes" and the "prince of the Arabs". I am sure many of you who tend to adore Óðinn may squirm a little about how negatively he is actually portrayed in many myths – especially in his thirst for the power that belongs to his norn, valkyria and goddess sisters; the power to rule fate.

One could indeed wonder if many of the stories are really about how male dominance came about: We also have an Edda poem, the Grǫttasǫngr, where two giantesses of great lineage and might are enslaved and forced to pull the millstone of destiny for "King Wisdom", and how they are abused until they start remembering their former glory as the creators of landscapes and of being the real powers behind the rotation of the earth and the millstone of fate, and begin to "grind" an ill fate and a destructive age for the sleep-walking king.

Another Edda poem, the Vǫlundarkvíða, tells of three valkyriur who arrive in their swan hides and live happily with their three husbands in the world of men until they vanish, and the three brothers are left to seek or wait for their return, all while the world suffers, ruled by the powers of greed and hatred, deteriorating into war, pestilence and natural disasters until the point of Ragnarǫk.

Nowadays, we moderns tend to think in terms of good and evil, and that a god must needs be perfect and above human fallibility. I do not mean to say that neither good nor evil exists, as such, but such polarity does not fit in Norse myths. They are made as allegories about the human spiritual path towards knowledge, and Óðinn, representing the spirit, the breath, and the one who causes the shifting of ages, also errs.

He is not an infallible god, he is the spirit in all that lives and breathes, all that seeks knowledge and learning, and which must go through trials and errors before learning to become wise. Sometimes, he will choose harmful paths because he thinks it will serve the greater good in the long run, and sometimes, the results are disastrous.

There is no question as to who the Edda poets sympathize with in these cases; they seem sternly on the side of the female victims, those whose powers have been usurped, allowing them to endlessly express their sorrows over the injustice and suffering caused by the power of men in this world, and especially by the powerful god Óðinn, who, in retrospect, is not above admitting his own guilt either.

STANZA 20: THE GODS AND GODDESSES WANT ANSWERS

20.Margs of frágu máltíþ yfir Heimdall há goþ, haurgar Loka, spár eþa spakmál sprund ef kendi, undorn of fram, unz nam húma.	20. Of manyfold great tidings they asked during the banquet the high gods asked Heimdallr the Shrines (goddesses) asked Loki; if prophecies or wise speech had issued from (Iðunn/Ora- cle) all day they asked until twilight approached

In stanza 20, the gods and goddesses want to know what the three gods, Heimdallr, Loki and Bragi, have learned from the oracle Iðunn, expecting prophecies and wise speech. The gods ask Heimdallr, while the goddesses, referred to in a heiti for goddesses; hörgar, "shrines", prefer to ask Loki, perhaps because Loki is half-woman. They keep asking, and what they want to know is whether the oracle, Iðunn, has offered up prophecies and wise speech, as they would have expected.

STANZA 21: THE ERRAND WAS FRUITLESS

21.Illa letu ordit hafa eyrindisleysu, oflítilfræga; vant at væla verda myndi, svá af svanna svars of gæti.	21. Badly, they were blamed for their fruitless errand of little glory Hard to engineer it so that they could get an answer to the riddle from the Swan/Woman (Iðunn/Oracle)

When the gods and goddesses realize that the journey to the oracle beneath the tree has been fruitless, or that the message has come in a riddle that they cannot solve, they get angry with the messengers. Iðunn is here called svanna – swan.

This is a common heiti for woman or goddess, and is an allusion to the norns or the valkyriur. In the Gylfaginning, Snorri lets slip that "swans" are dwelling in the Well of Origin, the very well from which norns rise to follow their individual human beings through life, spinning our fates. In the Vǫlundarkvíða, the three fate-spinning valkyriur wear the hides of swans.

STANZA 22: SEEKING NEW COUNSEL

22.Ansar Ómi, allir hlýddo: „Nótt skal nema nýræda til, hugsi til myrgins, hverr sem orkar rád til leggia rausnar ásom!"	22. Ómi * (Óðinn) replied They all listened "Night shall be used for new counsels Let each ponder, who is able, until morning so as to provide counsel to the benefit of the Aesir."

Ómi is a heiti for Óðinn which appears in the Grímnismál and the Gylfaginning. It may mean "Loud One" (from ON ómun – "loud") or else "Superior One" (from IE *auhuma). In this stanza, the god suggests that everybody spend the night trying to figure out the best counsel in this case. Perhaps they are trying to solve a riddle posed by the oracle, such as the reference to her tears of grief, her silence, and the verse suggesting Ragnarǫk being imminent. Perhaps they are trying to figure out how to deal with the problem caused by Iðunn's absence and the subsequent danger of death or Ragnarǫk.

Or perhaps they are trying to figure out why she is grieving so. In any case, Iðunn's refusal to allow the gods to see their future fate is obviously a problem, just as we saw that Iðunn's absence caused a problem in the other versions.

Stanza 23: Leaving the Banquet of the Gods

23.Rann meþ raustum Rindar móþr fóþrlarþr Fenris valla; gengu frá gildi goþin, qvöddo Hropt ok Frigg, sem Hrímfaxa fór.	23. Ran with the voices, Rind's abodes She and the tired wolf's father (Loki) left the feast The gods left the banquet and spoke farewell Hroptr (Óðinn) and Frigg ascended with Frost-Mane*

In this stanza, everyone leaves the party. The two first to leave are Loki together with Rindr, although in some translations, it is Rind's otherwise unknown mother. Rindr is mentioned in the Vegtamskvíða, where she is the fated mother of Vali, named after the vál, those who are chosen for an afterlife of resurrection, and who is destined to avenge his brother Baldr by "bringing Strife the Blind to the pyre". Her name may derive from rinda – to reject – a meaning that finds an explanation in Saxo Grammaticus' tale of how Vali was conceived: In this story, Óðinn had learned (from the vǫlva in the underworld) that Baldr would be avenged by Vali, and that his mother would be Rindr.

Rindr is a human woman, so the god enters the world of men in order to beget the destined child, but Rindr rejects him with great force. Then Óðinn tricks her and rapes her. In another Edda poem, the Gróagaldr, we learn that Rindr learned a spell from the ocean giantess Rán ("Robbery"), namely how to rid herself of the burdens she carries due to someone else's wrongdoing. While everybody are discussing, Rindr and Loki leaves the party together. The other gods follow, while Óðinn and Frigg join the horse Hrímfaxi ("Frost Mane"), who pulls the Moon god through the sky, suggesting that they are leaving into the night. Óðinn is called by his heiti Hroptr, which means "the shattered one".

This is also the name he assumes in the Sígrdrífumál, st. 13, in the description of how he embodied and released the runes into the world:

13.Hvgrvnar scaltv kvnna, ef þv vilt hveriom vera geðsvinnari gvma; þęr of réð, þęr of reist, þęr vm hvgði Hroptr af þeim legi, er leciþ hafdi or havsi Heiddravpniss oc or horni Hoddrofnis.	13.Soul-Runes you must know if you want to be wiser than most people: They were ruled They were carved Through the Shattered One's soul they ran From the juice that had emerged from the skull of Bright Drops and the Horn of Treasure-Shattering

STANZA 24: DAWN RISES

24.Dýrum settan Dellings maugr ió fram keyrdi iarknasteinom; mars of manheim maun af glóar, dró leik Dvalins drösull í reid.	4.Delling's*son (Day) urged on his steed (it was dawning), drove forward his horse adorned with ocean- stones The horse's mane shines From there over the whole world of men The steed, with his chariot Pulled Dvalin's* Lover (the Sun)

This stanza seems to be a poetical description of dawn, personified in the mythical being Dagr, whose name means "Day". He is the son of Dellingr, whose name means "opening between skies", otherwise known as the husband of Sól, the sun goddess, so Dagr is probably also the son of the Sun. In this stanza, it is Day's steed who pulls the Sun goddess, who is poetically referred to as Dvalins Leika – the "Hibernation's Lover".

Stanza 25: The Powers of Darkness Rest

<table>
<tr><td>

25.Iormungrundar
í iodyr nyrdra
und rót yztu
aðalþollar
gengu til reckio
gýgiur ok þursar,
náir, dvergar
ok döckálfar.

</td><td>

25. The Grand Ground (of giants)
to the Northern border
beneath the outermost root
of the Noble Tree (Yggdrasill)
- now went to rest;
Giantesses and thurses,
dead men, dwarves
and dark elves.

</td></tr>
</table>

In this verse, the emergence of daylight causes the powers of darkness, giantesses, thurses, the dead, dwarves and dark elves, to rest for a while.

Stanza 26: Ragnarǫk is Due

<table>
<tr><td>

26.Riso raknar,
rann álfraudull,
nordr at niflheim
nióla sótti;
upp nam ár Giöll
Úlfrúnar nidr,
hornþytvalldr
Himinbiarga.

</td><td>

26.The Great Ones (gods)arose
Alfrǫðull* (The Sun) ran
Darkness went north
towards Níflheimr (Misty World/Hel)
Wolf Rune's son (Heimdallr)
lifted up the Resounder (Gjallarhorn)
The Mighty Ruler of the Horn (Heim-
dallr) blew from the Heavenly Moun-
tains.*

</td></tr>
</table>

As soon as Day arrives and the Sun runs across the sky, the darkness goes north towards the realm of death. It could almost seem as if everything is now moving towards something better – that the powers of darkness are resting, vanishing into the oblivion of death. Yet, Heimdallr must lift up his Gjallarhorn, and he is now referred to as the son of the giantess called Wolf Rune – one of his nine mothers, and a reminder of the mortality of the universe itself.

When The Great World blows the resounding horn, Snorri explains, this means that he is warning of an attack from the destructive powers who want to destroy the world that the gods created at Ragnarǫk, and that the great battle is about to start, the one where the present world must die, and when the old gods are destined to die. The gods are no longer immortal after Iðunn's fall; they must die and leave the new world to come over to their children, who will instigate the new world from the place called Iðavǫllr.

The poem as we know it ends here, but the manuscript was defect in the end, and there may have been more verses that are now missing. This is, however, all that we have left.

Nordisch-Germanische Götter und Helden re-published in 1887 as Unzre Vorzeit by Wilhelm Wagner and Jakob Nover

-Authors Note: Carl Emil Doepler: Heimdallr Demands the Release of Iðunn from Hel (another possible take on the Iðunn myth was that Hel refused to let her return to the gods, just as she kept Balder. I could not find any direct evidence for this in the text, but it is not a bad guess).-

Summary

To sum up the Iðunn myth as it is presented in the Hrafnagaldr:

1. Iðunn is charged with guarding the mead of poetry. In this, she is likened to Urðr, the norn of origins, and with the ultimate power over destiny. Iðunn's likeness to Urðr is obvious; While Urðr makes sure that the universe "tree" is nurtured with the power of eternal rejuvenation and resurrection, countering the powers of death and decay that also eats off the "tree", so Iðunn makes sure that the gods are nurtured with the power of renewal and resurrection from ageing and death. Both beings reside in a place of origins, associated with "water-sources". Iðunn is clearly assuming the role of "the Maiden with the Mead", the woman who dwells in a golden abode mysteriously situated in the darkest depths of Hel, surrounded by dangerous paths and destructive giants, yet her mead and her embrace is the key to resurrection from death.

2. Iðunn "falls", for unexplained reasons, down to the trunk of the universal tree, and is very unhappy about it. This is the parallel to the Haustlǫng and Skaldskaparmál versions where she is abducted by the giant of death and brought to the Drumming World. She is "wed to the shrines" and given a wolf-hide, with which she lets herself go, changes her nature, plays with illusion and changes her shape.

3. Óðinn charges a trinity of gods, Heimdallr, Bragi and Loki, to seek the goddess in the underworld, where they expect her to have assumed the role of an oracle who will counsel them about future challenges. The trinity echoes earlier trinity myths where the three gods travel together, instigating something new. Here, the storyline differs from the other two, where the trinity appear before Iðunn "falls", where the gods immediately grow old, and where Loki alone is sent to rescue Iðunn with the help of Freyia's bird hide.

4. The three gods must sing galdrar (spell-songs), ride on gandr (magical wands) and meditate in a "seat of visions" in order to reach the goddess in the underworld.

5. The Oracle, Iðunn, refuses to let them in on the secrets of the future, instead showing them how sorrowful she is, weeping red tears. There is a sense of doom, of Ragnarǫk being imminent.

6. The three gods return to find Óðinn having taken up the high seat in a hall that otherwise would have belonged to the goddesses. The valkyriur are still serving the precious mead of resurrection, but are now ruled by Óðinn, who is greeted as the ruler of the mead of the high seat. He is, however, also referred to as a harm-worker, a reference to how he stole the mead of poetry from its rightful guardian, the giantess who stayed weeping behind in the underworld while he returned to life with a well of new knowledge and power. There is a strong sense of Óðinn somehow being guilty of causing the present state of doom.

7. The messengers admit that for all their efforts, they have not received the esoteric knowledge that the fallen goddess alone possesses, and are blamed for this failure. Everybody leave the hall of the goddesses with the night itself.

8. Things appear to be going well, with the powers of darkness seemingly leaving the world as the day dawns, but then, Heimdallr lifts his resounding horn to warn that Ragnarǫk is at large. Somehow, this is the ultimate consequence of the fall of the goddess who rules over immortality; that the gods who hold the present world together are doomed to finally die.

As I finished translating and analyzing the Hrafnagaldr, I was increasingly convinced that the poem belongs with the other Edda poems, referring to known lore of the Edda even while some parts seem obscure because we lack knowledge of the complete lore that once existed. If it is indeed a late poem by someone who knew Edda lore well, then that person had really done the homework, and understood, perhaps, more about the ancient lore than any 19th to 20th century student may ever hope to grasp.

Primary Sources

Part 1: Skaldskaparmál

Snorri Sturluson:
•Gylfaginning (Prose Edda)
•Skaldskaparmál (Prose Edda)
•Ynglinga saga (Heimskringla)
Prose Edda: https://heimskringla.no/wiki/Edda_Snorra_Sturlusonar
-Gylfaginning: https://heimskringla.no/wiki/Gylfaginning
-Skaldskaparmál: https://heimskringla.no/wiki/Sk%C3%A1ldskaparm%C3%A1l
Heimskringla: https://heimskringla.no/wiki/Heimskringla
-Ynglinga saga: https://heimskringla.no/wiki/Ynglinga_saga
Simek, Rudolf: «Dictionary of Northern Mythology"
Faulkes, Antony: "Edda Snorri Sturluson»

Part 2: Haustlǫng

Finnúr Jónsson (1912): https://heimskringla.no/wiki/Den_norsk-islandske_skjaldedigtning
-Haustlǫng: https://heimskringla.no/wiki/Haustl%C3%B6ng
Faulkes, Antony; «Edda Snorri Sturluson»

Part 3: Hrafnagaldr Óðins eða Forspjallsljóð

The Poetic Edda
-Bugge, Sophus (ed.) (1867): Sæmundar Edda https://etext.old.no/
-Hrafnagaldr: https://etext.old.no/Bugge/forspjal.html

Translations of the Hrafnagaldr:

Lassen, Anette (2011): http://www.vsnrweb-publications.org.uk/Text%20Series/Hrafnagaldur%20Odins.pdf

Thorpe, Benjamin (1865): http://www.germanicmythology.com/works/ThorpeEdda/thorpe04.html

Eysteinn Björnsson and William P.Reeves (1998): http://web.archive.org/web/20020605081728/http://www.hi.is/~eybjorn/ugm/hrg/main.html

LIST OF MATRONAE (SOURCE: RUDOLF SIMEK "DICTIONARY OF NORTHERN MYTHOLOGY")

Abiamarcae/Ambiamarcae (Borderland Mothers)
Inscriptions: "Matronis Abiamarcis". "Matronibus Ambiorenesibus"
Where: Floisdorf near Aachen, West Germany (2)
Meaning: Abiamarcae = "Land Beyond" (or "Borderland March"). Ambiamarca = "People of the Marches. Matronis Abiamarcis: "Mothers to the March/Rhine people".

Abirenae (River Mothers)
Inscription: "Matronis Abirenibus"
Where: Deutz, West Germany (1)
Meaning: Abirenae= "Of the Rhine Borderland". Matronis Ambirenae= "Mothers of the Rhine People"

Afliae (Powerful, Creative Mothers)
Inscriptions: "Matronis Afliabus". "Matronis Aflims"
Where: Cologne, Germany (2)Meaning: Afliae = (ON: Afla= "power", "procreation"): Matronis Afliabus: "To The Powerful, Procreative Mothers"

Ahinehiae (Mothers Of the River)
Meaning: Ahinehiae – from OHG "aha": "Water, River" – "The River Mothers"
Where: Blankenheim, near Aachen, West Germany (1)

Ahueccaniae (Prophetic Magic Water Women
Inscriptions:"Ahueccanis Avehae et Hellivesae"
Meaning: "Prophetic Magic Water Beings"
-*ahwo, OHG "aha" – "Water", "River"
-*wiccian, AngloSaxon – "To Conjure", "Do Magic"
- *wicken, MHG – "To Prophecy"
Where: Gleuel, Cologne, Germany (1) (dated to 201.A.D)

Alaferhviae (Great, Life-Giving Mothers)
Inscriptions: "Matronibus Alaferhiviabus"
Meaning: Either: "The Great Life Giving Mothers" (*ferh
(OHG)/*feorh (AngloSaxon)= "life") or is else derived from
*fereheih (OHG) = "tree, oak", when we get: "The Mothers
Belonging to All Trees" (Trees are metaphors for people and
lineages) or "The Mothers Belonging to All Oaks" (Oak is a
female tree, symbolizing woman, so that the meaning could
be "The Mothers of All Mothers" (of lineages).Where: Jülich,
West Germany (several)

Alagabiae (All-Giving Mothers)
Inscriptions: "Matronis Alagabius"
Meaning: "Mothers Who Give Everything"
Where: Bürgel, Solingen, West Germany, fourth century AD
(1)
Thought to be a Germanic counterpart to the partially
Celticized matron name Ollogabiae. It is possible that the
same matrons were venerated under both names among the
mixed Germanic-Celtic population on the lower Rhine.

Alaisiagae (Venerated Mothers)
Inscriptions: "Duabus Alaisiabis, Baudihillia et Friagabis",
"Duabus Alaisiabis, Beda et Fimmilena", "Duabus Alaisiabis
et Thingus"
Meaning: "The Two Venerated Ones" (identified as
Baudihilla/Beda and Friagabis/Fimmilena) in one instance
associated with "Thingus" – Mars (the god of war).

The names of the Two Venerated Ones, Baudihilla/Beda and Friagabis/Fimmilena has been associated with the Frisian law terms Bodthing and Fimelthing – "Summon" and "Sentence", and even when studied on their own the names indicate that the Two Venerated Ones were closely related to a court of justice, and that they may have been goddesses of law and justice.Where: Housesteads on Hadrian's Wall (Cumbria) (3 inscriptions)

Alateivia (The All Divine One)
Inscription: "Alateiviae ex iussu Divos medicus"
Meaning: "To The All Divine One, on her own command, from the physician Divos" – possibly a goddess of healing.
Where: Xanten (1)

Alaterviae (All Loyal/Oak Tree Mothers)
Inscriptions: "Matribus Alatervis (et Matribus Campestribus)"
Meaning: "The All-Loyal Mothers (and the Countryland(?)... (?) Mothers)" or "The Mothers of the Oak Trees" (Oak trees=women, lineages)
Where: Edinburgh

Albiahenae (Mothers of Albiniacum)
Meaning: Possibly connected to the place Albiniacum. Mothers connected to that place and its people.
Where: Ober-Elvenich, Euskirchen, West Germany
Alhiahenae (Temple/Oak Mothers)
Inscriptions: "Matronis Alhiahenabus"
Meaning: "Mothers of the Temples"/"Mothers of Oaks" (Oak= feminine tree=Woman, Ancestress, Lineage)
Where: Neidenstein, Heidelberg

Almaviaheniae (Elm Path Mothers)
Where: Cologne
Meaning: Associated with the river Elm (OHG: Elmaha) or to the tree-sort elm. Possibly a Celtic origin: The "Matrae Almahae" – suggesting a Celtic origin to the name. (Elm=feminine tree=Woman, Ancestress, Lineage)

Alusneihae (Beer Mothers)
Where: Inden-Pier, Kreis Düren, West Germany (2)
Meaning: From Gmc «aluþ» -- «Beer», «Intoxicating Drink»
-- the second part of the name is uncertain, but is possibly
the same as the mysterious "neha" in the goddess name
Nehallennia: Is it from LAT *nex, *necare – "To Kill", or from
the verb "helan" – "To Hide", or from Gmc *neu – associated
with words for seafaring or approximation ("Mothers of Beer
Approaching", "Mothers of Beer Ships" or something along
that line).

**Ambiamarcae/ Ambiomarciae (Mothers of the
Fenced in Marchlands)**
Inscription (LAT) in votive altar at Deutz (dated 252 AD):
"In honorem domus divinae et genio loci, Ambiamarcis,
Ambiorenesibus, Marti Victori, Mercurio, Neptuno, Cereri,
diis deabusque omnibus"
("In Honor of the divine house and the protective spirits
of this place, the Ambiamarcae (Mothers), Ambiorenis
(Mothers), the victorious Mars (god of war), Mercury (god of
divine messages), Neptun (god of oceans), Ceres (goddess of
Earth), and all the gods and goddesses")
Where: Deutz (1), Wardt, West Germany (dated 218 AD)
(1), Remagen (1): "et Genio loci, Marti, Herculi, Mercurio,
Ambiomarcis" ("and the protective spirits, Mars, Hercules
(Thor), Ambiomarcae")
Meaning: The name may be related to a particular place
called Ambia (Embt today). The name seems to be a Celtic-
Germanic mixed formation with strong Roman influence
(although the names Mars, Mercury, Neptun and Ceres and
Hercules would have been used in Latin for the gods Týr,
Odin, Njord and Frigg/Freyia and Thor).

Ambiorenses (Mothers of Both Sides)
Where: Deutz (1)
Meaning: "Mothers of Both Sides of the Rhine" (ancestral mothers to people on both sides, perhaps both Celts and Germans, or of two tribes).
Amfratninae (Mothers of Success)
Where: Eschweiler, Germany (12)
Meaning: OHG *frad – "capable", *fradi – "efficiency", "success"

Amnesahenae
Inscription: «Matronis Amnesahenis»
Where: Cologne, Germany
Meaning: Probably Celtic name

Andrusteinhiae (The Mother Followers)
Where: Bonn, Godesberg, Cologne (3)
Meaning: Old Franconian "antrustio"- "follower", same meaning as ON "fylgja" – a female guardian spirit and ancestral mother to a particular lineage or tribe.

Anesiaminehae (The Mothers of the River Anesus)
Where: Zülpich (1)
Meaning: The name is possibly Celtic and refers to rhe river name Anesus, Anasus (nowadaysEnns) which is however far away from the situation of the find (could be due to migrations, an ancestral mother of a tribe connected to the River Anesus having moved on). Otherwise uncertain meaning.

Annaneptiae (The Favorable/Generous Kinswomen Mothers)
Inscription: «Matribus Annaneptis»
Where: Xanten (233 AD) (1)
Meaning: LAT "Matres" – "Mothers", OHG "Unnan" – "To Grant"/Gothic "ansts" – "favour", and ON "Nipt" – "Sister", "Female Relative", "Kinswomen" – the name Annaneptiae meaning "Mothers (of/who are) Granting/Favorable/Generous Sisters/Kinswomen". (Kinswomen could here also mean followers, spirit beings, ancestral mother souls who guard and protect and grant favors to their descendants).

Arvagastiae (Arwagasti's Mothers)
Inscription: "Matronis Arvagastis"
Where: Müddersheim near Aachen, West Germany (150 AD)
(1)
Meaning: From the Germanic personal name *Arwagasti
(Franconian Arbogastes, Arvagastes, 4th/5th century).
(My interpretation: Possibly the ancestral mothers of a
particular clan, either with a male ancestor called Arwagasti
or with a male descendant called Arwagasti who raised the
altar to his clan-mothers.)

Arvolecia (Goddess of Quick Healing)
Inscription: "Deae Arvolecie"
Where: Brough, England (150 AD) (1)
Meaning: Arvolecia is probably a Germanic name and
perhaps means "The Quick Healer". The goddess votive altar
was raised by one Maiotius in 150 AD England – his name is
Celtic. Celtic-German overlapping was very common at this
time.

Asericinehae (Mothers of the Ancestral Reign)
Inscription: "Matronis Asericinehabus", "Matronis
Aserecinehis"
Where: at Odenhausen ("Odins Houses") and Odendorf
("Odins Place") in Cologne, Germany (3)
Meaning: Possibly related to the Germanic personal name
*Ansu-rik, according to Simek's Dictionary of Northern
Mythology. Thus they could represent the ancestral mothers
of a person called Ansurik and his lineage. But the name
Ansurik/Ansoricus means "Ancestral Reign". I think the
name of the goddess collective thus could mean "Mothers of
the Ancestral Reign".

**Audrinehae (Mothers of Divine Support - Mothers of
Destiny)**
Inscriptions: "Matronis Audrinehae" (4), "M.Auðrinehae" (1),
"M.Authrinaheae" (1), "M.Autrinahenae" (1)
Where: Hermühlheim, Cologne (Germany) (7)
Meaning: Proto-Norse *auja – "divine protection", or ON
"auða" – "destiny", "fate"

Aufanie (Goddess(es) of Sacred Abundance)
Inscriptions: Nearly 90 inscriptions are dedicated to the singular "Deae Aufaniae" (Goddess Aufania) or "Sanctae Aufania" (Sacred Aufania) or else the plural "Matronis Aufaniabus" (Aufania-Mothers).
Where: They are found around Bonn, Nettersheim, Cordoba/Spain and Lyon/France, and at the Lower Rhine, dating between 164 AD-235 AD and particularly numerous around the year 200 AD.
Meaning: Aufanie suggests "generous ancestral mother" from Gothic "ufjo" – "abundance"

Aumenahae (Mothers of the River Aumenau)
Inscriptions: "Matronis" or "Matribus Aumenahenis"
Where: Cologne, Germany (2)
Meaning: Connected to the river name Oumena/Aumenau near Ems and der Lahn.

Austriahenae (Mothers of the Eastern Tribes)
Inscriptions: "Matronis Austriahenis"
Where: More than 150 votive stones from the cult of matrons were found in Morken-Harff, all except one was dedicated to the these mothers.
Meaning: "The Eastern Ones" (like the "Austri/Ostro" in Ostrogoths: "The Eastern Goths")

Aviatinehae
Inscription: "Matronis Rumanehis item Aviatinehis" ("To the Rumanehae mothers and the Aviatinehae")
Where: Bürgel, Solingen, West Germany
Meaning: Uncertain

Axisinginehae (Mothers of the Grain Ears)
Where: Cologne (1)
Meaning: Related to Gothic "ahs" – "ear" of grain.

Baduhenna (Goddess of Battle)
Where: Frisia.
Source: Tacitus, in his "Annales", IV, 73) writes that a grove in Frisia was dedicated to Baduhenna and that 900 Roman soldiers were slaughtered near this grove in 28 AD.
Meaning: Cognate with *batwa – "battle", and "-henae", which is uncertain in meaning but often a part of German matron names, possibly having the meaning of "goddess" or "matron".

Berguiahenae (Oak Mothers, Mountain Mothers)
Inscriptions: "Matronis Berhuiahenis" "...rguiahenis", "...B.. guinehis"
Where: Gereonsweiler, Jülich, Germany (2) and Tetz near Aachen (1).
Meaning: Possibly related to OHG "fereheih" – "oak", but uncertain meaning. I wonder if the ON "bergr" – "mountain" could be a possible association.

Borvoboendoa
Where: Utrecht (2)
Meaning: Celtic (means I don't know)

Boudunnehae
Where: Cologne (2)
Meaning: Celtic

Burorina (The Provider Goddess)
Where: Walcheren (1)
Meaning: From Anglo-Saxon "byrele" – "giver". The meaning of her name is cognate with Celtic/Germanic goddess Rosmerta (The Great Provider) and the Norse goddess name for Freyia, Gefion/Gefn (The Provider). Very common meaning of many important goddess names.

Caimineae
Where: Euskirchen, Germany (1)
Meaning: Unknown. Possibly Celtic.

Cantrusteihiae (Mothers of the Condrusi Tribe)
Four 2nd and third century votive stones.
Meaning: Unknown, possibly Celtic and derived from the tribal name Condrusi.

Chandrumanehae
Where: Billig near Euskirchen, Germany (1)
Meaning: Unknown

Ethrahenae (Mothers of the Fences/Borders)
Where: Wollersheim and Rödingen (2)
Meaning: OHG "ettar" -- fence", "border".

Euthungae (Mothers of the Suebi Luthungi Tribe)
Inscription: "Matribus Suebis Euthungabus"
Where: Cologne (1)
Meaning: From the tribe Luthungi, one of the Suebian tribes.
These mothers were obviously tribal ancestral mothers.

Fernovineae (Mothers of the Old Rivers)
Inscriptions:"Matronis Fernovineis/Fernovinehis"
Where: Meckenheim and Cologne (2)
Meaning: *fern-awi – "Old Stream"

Frisavae (Mothers of the Frisian Ancestors)
Inscription: "Matribus Frisavis Paternis" (To the Mothers of
the Frisian Ancestors)
Where: Wissen, near Xanten, Germany
Meaning: Matres (LAT): "Mothers", Frisavae= "Of the Frisian
(tribe)", "Paternis (LAT)="Ancestors"

Gabiae (The Generous Mothers)
Inscription: At least ten votive stones dedicated to "Matronis
Gabiabus", and one saying "Iunonibus Gabiabus" iunones is
Latin and means the same as matrons – "mothers", ancestral
mothers)
Where: Rövenich near Euskirkchen, Germany
Meaning: Cognate with the ON goddess name Gefion (Gefn,
Freyia): Generous, Giving, Providing

Gamaleda (The Old Great Grandmother Goddess)
Inscription dedicated to the "Ammacae sive Gamaledae" on
votive altar
Where: Maastrich, Netherlands (1)
Meaning: Gamaleda is related to ON "gamall" – "old" and
ON "Edda" – "Great Grandmother". (Ammaca is a Gaulish
goddess)

Gantunae (The Goose Women)
Inscriptions: "Gantunis Flossia Paterna" (Goose Women,
Ancestral Mothers of the Flosi Tribe)
Where: Cologne, Germany (1)
Meaning: *ganta = "goose" (associated with an ancient cult of
water birds and water bird goddesses common in both Indo-
European and Finno-Ugric traditions)
Garmangabis (The Great Generous Giver Goddess)
Where: Durham, North England (1) dated 238-244 AD.
The votive stone was set up by members of the Suebi tribe
stationed there.

Gavadiae (The Goddesses of Pledges)
Inscriptions: Eight votive stones from around 200 AD
dedicated to the "Matronis Gavadiabus".
Where: Jülich (6), Mönchengradbach (2)
Meaning: Related to Gothic "wadi" = "pledge" and
"gawadijon" – "betroth". Goddesses of either vows and oaths
or matchmaking.

Gavasiae (The Clothing Mothers)
Inscriptions: "Matronis Gavasiabus"
Where: Cologne (1)
Meaning: Gothic "gawasjon" – "clothe", thought to refer
to the making of swaddling clothes for a baby (midwifery).
Seeing as women provided clothing in general, I think the
name could just refer to the essentially female function of
protecting and providing people with clothing.

Matres Germanae (The Mothers of the Germans)
Inscription: "Matribus meis Germanis Suebis", "Matribus
Italis Germanis Gallis Britis"
Where: Cologne (2)
Meaning: "German" (and Italian, Gallic and British), Mothers
of the People.

Deae Gratichae (The Graticha Goddess)
Where: Euskirchen (several)
Meaning: Uncertain

Guinehae (The Guinehae Mothers)
Where: Tetz (1)
Meaning: Uncertain

Hamavehae (The Mothers of the Chamavi Tribe)
Where: Alrdorf (3)
Meaning: The name is thought to be derived from the tribal
name Chamavi

**Dea Hariasa (The Ruler Goddess or the Goddess of
Rulers)**
Where: Cologne (1) 187 AD
Meaning: Related to the ON word for "ruler" – heri, or "to
rule" – heria, etymologically connected to a valkyria name:
Herja ("To Rule")

Havae (The High Mothers)
Where: Merzenich near Düren.
Meaning: Semantically close to the ON word for "High" –
"háva"/"hárr"

Hiannanefae
Thought to be the same as the Kannanefates
Hiannanefatae
Thought to be the same as the Kannanefates

Hiheriaiae (The Jay Bird Mothers)
Where: Enzen near Euskirchen (1)
Meaning: From Old Germanic*hihera – "jay"

Deae Hurstaergae (The Hurstaerga Goddesses)
Where: Tiel/Holland (2nd/3rd century AD)
Meaning: Unknown

**Dea Idbangabia (The Hard Working Provider
Goddess)**
Where: Pier, Düren/Germany (1)
Meaning: Possibly from Idiangabia, ON:Iðinn = hard
working, OHG Gabia = ON: Gefia – "to give", "to provide"
(like in the goddess name Gefion)

Iulineihiae (The Mothers of Juliacum)
Where: Müntz near Jülich
Meaning: From the name of the town Juliacum (= Jülich)

Kannanefates (The Mothers of the Ancestors of the Cannanefatium Regiment)
Inscription: "Matribus paternis Kannanefatibus"
Where: Cologne
Meaning: The XXX legion of the Roman army was called the Canennefatium, and this inscription seems to have been made by Germanic or Celtic soldiers of the Roman army who call on the protection of their ancestral mothers – now the mothers of the regiment.

Leudinae (The Mothers of Leudiacum)
Where: Derichsweller near Düren
Meaning: From the town name Leudiacum or Leudium – possibly the same as present day Lüttich.

Mahalinehae (Mothers of the Justice Court)
Where: Cologne (2)
Meaning: Either from the place name Mecheln, or else to Germanic *mahal – "place of justice", "parliament"

Masanae (The Masanae Mothers)
Inscription: "Matribus Masanabus" ("To the Masanae Mothers")
Where: Cologne (1), Germany
Meaning: Uncertain

Deae Mediotautehae (Goddesses of the Midland)
Where: Cologne (1)
Meaning: "Midland" – possibly Celtic.

Dea Meduna (Goddess of Spring)
Where: Bad Betrich,Germany (1)
Meaning: Uncertain, possibly Celtic – probably to do with spring

Dea Menmanhia (Necklace Bearing Goddess (?)
Where: Rome, Italy
Meaning: Probably Germanic but uncertain meaning. (ON: Mén=Jewel, Necklace, Menia= "Servant girl", "Necklace Bearer")

Naitineae (River Mothers)
Where: Cologne
Meaning: Probably derived from the name of a river

Dea Nehalennia (Goddess of Seafaring (?), Goddess of Hidden Death (?)
Where: Domburg, Walcheren, Netherlands (28), Colijnsplaat, Nord-Beveland (28), Cologne, Germany (2) – about 58 inscriptions found to Nehalennia altogether
Meanings: From *neu – "ship", or else from "nex"/ "necare" = Death, To Kill, and *helan = hide

Nervinae (Mothers of the Nervi Tribe)
Where: Bavay, North France
Meaning: Derived from the Germanic tribe Nervii.

Ollogabiae (Mothers of Plentiful Provisions)
Where: Mainz (2) "Matronae Ollogabiae"
Meaning: A Celtic counterpart to the Germanic Alagabiae and roughly means the same

Ratheithiae (Mothers of the Fate Wheel)
Where: Euskirchen, Germany (1)
Meaning: Proto-Germanic *raþa, "wheel" (i.e. fate)

Dea Ricagambeda (The Strong Lady Goddess)
Where: Hadrian's Wall, North England "Deae Ricagambedae"
Meaning: Some different possibilities, but related -- Simek lands on the meaning "Strong Lady", which seems to best convey the sense of what is meant in any case.

Rumanehae/Romanehae (Mothers of the Roman Settlement)

Where: Lower Rhine around 200 AD, "Matrinos Rumanehis" (more than a dozen found)
Meaning: Mothers of Germanic peoples who lived in Roman settlements

Saithchamiae (Mothers of Magic)

Where: Hoven near Zülpich (2)
Meaning: Related to ON seiðr= magic, divination, witchcraft.

Dea Sandraudiga (Goddess of True Wealth)

Where: Zundert, Holland. "Deae Sandraudigae cultores temple"
Meaning: ON "sannr" – true, Gothic "audags" – "rich"

Seccanehae (Mothers of the Clan of Secchus)

Where: Aachen, Germany
Meaning: Perhaps related to the personal name Secchus

Dea Sibulca (Sibyl Goddess)

Where: Bonn
Meaning: Uncertain (to do with "sibylla"?)

Dea Sulevia (Goddess of Hot Springs)

Where: Trier (1)
Meaning: Uncertain, possibly related to goddess Sulis from Bath, England: "Goddess of Hot Springs"

Matronae Suleviae (Mothers of Hot Springs)

Where: More than forty inscriptions from all over the Roman Empire between 89 AD-160 AD
Meaning: Uncertain, possibly related to goddess Sulis from Bath, England: "Goddess of Hot Springs"

Dea Sunucsal/Sunuxal (Goddess of the Sunuci Tribe)

Where: Ten inscriptions from the Lower Rhine, one dated to 239 AD.
Meaning: Related to the German tribe Sunuci

Teniavehae (Mothers of Teniaveha)
Where: Blankenstein, Aachen, Germany (1)
Meaning: Possibly related to a place-name

Textumeihae (Mothers of the Gods of the Southern People)
Where: Several votive stones along the Lower Rhine
Meaning: Gutenbrunner related the name to meaning "gods of the southern people", perhaps from Gothic "taishwa", Old Irish "dess" – "right", "south", according to Birkhan it may mean "Bringers of Joy"

Dea Travalaeha (The Desired Goddess)
Where: Cologne, Germany (1)
Meaning: Connected with the name þrawija on the Swedish rune stone from Kalleby and with the Proto-Norse þrawo – "to long", "to desire"

Tummaestiae (Mothers of House Constructions)
Where: Sinzenich near Euskirchen, "Matronis Tumaestis"
Meaning: The Helping Goddesses of the House or the Building Site
Turstuahenae (Mothers of Trolls' Power)
Where: Derichsweiler, Düren, Germany (2), 2nd and 3rd centuries AD
Meaning: Probably from ON þurs – «thurse», «troll» (and OHG duris, thuris), also meaning "mighty". Some think it is from Gothic þaurstei – «thirst»

Udravarinehae /Udrovarinehae (Mothers of the Otter Dam)
Where: Lower Rhine (2)
Meaning: to do with otters and dams (associated with the many river mothers)

Ulauhinehae (Mothers of the Owl Grove / Mothers of the River Flow)

Where: Gleich near Füssensich (1)
Meaning: from *uwa-lauha – "Owl-Grove" or else from
*plau/pleu – "flow", hence "river goddess"

Vacallinehae (Mothers of the River Vahalis and the People of Vacall)

Where: Over 130 inscriptions from the 2nd and 3rd centuries
from the temple area at Pesch, Kreis Aachen and around that
area. Additionally, 10 inscriptions in another place and 150
fragmented inscriptions from around the same area that are
probably dedicated to the same goddesses.
Also: Vocallinehae, at Pesch, Germany (7)
Meaning: derived from the place name *Vacall – probably
the same as Wachendorf near Antweiler on the stream
Wachenbach, or else from the river name Waal/Vahalis.

Dea Vagdavercustis (Goddess of Warlike Virtues)

Where: Seven votive stones around the Lower Rhine,
Plumtonwall on Hadrian's wall in North England and one
from Hungary (!)
Meaning: "Warlike Virtue"

Vallabnaehiae/Vallamaeneihiae (Mothers of the Valamni clan)

Where: Cologne, Germany
Meaning: Related to the Celtic personal name Valamni

Vapthiae (The Vapthia Mothers)

Where: Lower Rhine after 150 AD)
Meaning: Uncertain

Vataranehae/Veteranehae¨(The Water Mothers)

Where: Embeken near Düren, Germany

Vatviae (The Clairvoyant Mothers)

Where: Rödingen (3), Morken-Haff (5), Germany
Meaning: Germanic "Water" or else from Latin "vates" –
"seer"

Dea Vercana (Goddess of Works, or Birch Goddess)
Where: Bad Betrich (1), Ernstweiler (1)
Meaning: *werka – "Work", or else the name of the b-rune, ON "bjarkan", from "birch". The birch played a role in folk medicine.

Vesuneiahenae (Mothers of Wisse)
Where: Vettweis (5)
Meaning: Possibly from the place Wisse, now Vettweiss.

Dea Vihansa (Goddess of Dedications or Goddess of Battle)
Where: Tongern in Belgium, a bronze plaque dedicating shield and spear to this goddess from a centurion of the III legion.
Meaning: Germanic *wihan – "to fight", or from *wihan – "to dedicate"

Viradecdis /Viradestis, Viratehis, Virodacthis (Goddess of Manly Virtue)
Where: Vechten (1), Birrens, North England (1), Lower Rhine (2), Trebur (1)
Meaning: From Celtic ferdaht – "masculinity"

Main source: Rudolf Simek "Dictionary of Northern Mythology"

Haustlǫng oversatt til norsk av Maria Kvilhaug

1.Hvorledes skal jeg besynge Thorleif, Skjoldets giver ?
Jeg ser på det blanke skjoldets rand
tre kraftige guders
og Slavebinderens (Þjazi's)
svikefulle tilstedeværelse

2. Den Veltalende Kvinnens Ulv (Tjatse)
fløy med glam og vingeflapping
for u-kort (lang) tid siden
til Sagnenes Fortellere (æsene)
På seg hadde han den urgamle
skikkelsen til den årsgamle (ørnen)

Ørnen satte seg i tidenes begynnelse
der Æsene bar næring til jordovnen
Bergenes Givende Kvinnes (jotunkvinnens)
Borg-Dyr (jotnen = Tjatse)
var ingen blaut feiging.

3. Delvis Ublandet Svik (Tjatse)
var sen til å starte gudenes måltid
Den Hjelmkledte Giver av Veltalenhet til Gudene (Odin)
mente at noen sto bak dette.

Den Veldig Kloke Bølgenes Måke-Innvollers Lik-Kaster (Tjatse)
snakket fra Det Urgamle Treet (Yggdrasill).
Hænirs venn (Loke) likte ham dårlig

4. Fjellhyleren (ulven = Tjatse)
spurte Brynjestigeren (Hænir eller en av de andre gudene)
om å dele med seg en del
av det hellige måltid *

Ravnegudens (Odins) Venn (Loke)
måtte blåse på ilden

Den Krigshungrige Herskeren av Vennskapets Vogn (Tjatse) lot seg stige ned fra
oven
til der Gudenes Lojale Beskyttere (æsene)
hadde ankommet.

5. Jordas Anstendige Herre (Odin)
befalte øyeblikkelig
at Farbautes Sønn (Loke) skulle dele
det Trommende Beltes Gudinnes Hval (oksen)
med Tjenestemannen (Tjatse)

Og den Bragd-Vise Gudenes Oppvigler (Loke)
delte nå oksen (offeret) i fire
opp fra det brede bordet (alteret)

6. Og den Sultne Jotunkvinnens Far (Tjatse)
spiste grådig av Eikerøttenes Tamme Bjørn (oksen)
dette var for lenge siden –

før den Dype Sjelens Gjemte Dyr (Loke)
slo til Krigs-Trofeet (Tjatse) med en stokk;
Han slo Jordas Mektige Fiende (Tjatse)
fra oven, mellom skuldrene.

7. Da ble Sigyns Armers Byrde* (Loke)
 - han sm alle guder oppfatter som i lenker –
bundet fast til Skigudinnens Fosterfar* (Tjatse)

Stokken var limt fast til
Jotunheimenes Spøkelse (Tjatse)
og hendene til Hænirs Trofaste Venn (Loke) var limt fast til stangen.

8. Flokkens Åtselfugl (Tjatse)
var glad for sin fangst
og fløy langt avgårde
med den Kyndige Guden (Loke)
slik at Ulvens Far (Loke)
var i ferd med å rives i sund

Da tigget Tors Venn (Loke)
om nåde fra Jotnens Barn (Tjatse)
For alle sine krefter
var den Tunge Luften (Loke)
i ferd med å bryte sammen

9. Hymirs Ætte-Tre (Tjatse) spurte
Fortellingenes Beveger* (Loke)
som var gal av smerte –
om han kunne bringe til ham
Møya som Kjenner Æsenes Alders-Kur (Iðunn)

De Flammende Guders Belte-Tyv* (Loke)
bragte da
Kilde-Slettenes Benkers Gudinne (Iðunn)
til Stein-Herskeren Nedenfor (Tjatse)
sine gårder.

10. De Bratte Fjellenes Beboere (jotnene)
var ikke så veldig triste (var veldig glade)
for at Iðunn hadde kommet
fra sør (Åsgård ligger i sør) til jotnene

Alle Yngve-Frøys Ætter (gudene)
aldrende og gråhårede
gikk til tinget

Herskerne var ellers
ganske stygge å se på nå

11. Helt til de (gudene) fant
Øl-Giverens (Iðunns)
Flommende Lik-Sjøs Blodhund (Loke)
og bandt tyven,
Svikets Tre (Loke), som hadde ledet
Øl-Giveren (Iðunn) på ville veier.

«Du skal lide forferdelig, Loke,»
slik talte Den Sinte (Tor)
«om du ikke bringer tilbake den
Dyrebare Møya som Øker Gudenes Glede (Iðunn)!»

12. Jeg har hørt dette
at Hønirs (tankenes) Intensjons-Tester (Loke)
senere lurte tilbake
Æsenes Elskerinne (Iðunn).

Han fløy vekk i en hauks skikkelse
og Jotunkvinnens Far (Tjatse),
den raske, vinge-flappende Konge-Lureren
fulgte med Ørne-Sug (vind, dødelighet)
etter Haukens Barn (Loke).

13. Treverket begynte å brenne
det som De Hellige Makter
hadde gjort til brensel.

Og Sønnen til Han Som Frir til Hun Som Griper (Tjatse)
brant.

Brått endte hans reise.
(...)

Special Addtion

MARIA KVILHAUG'S HAND DRAWN COMIC STRIP

The Story Of Iðunn

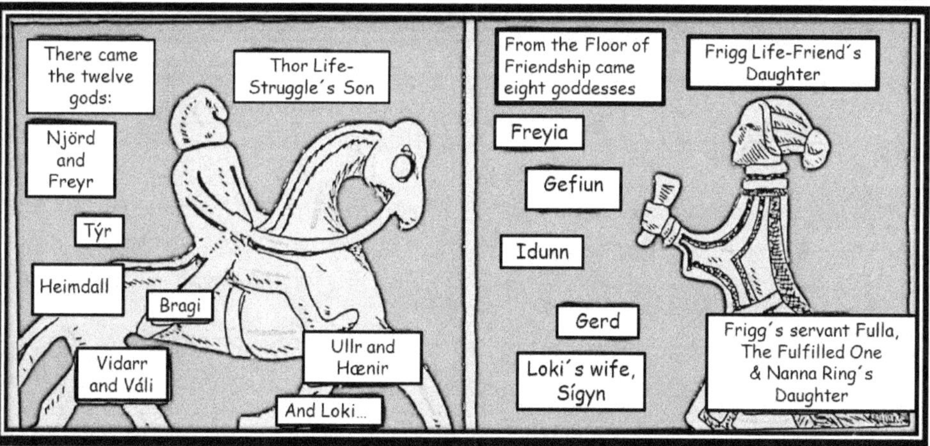

Bragi, the master skáld, sat next to the terrifying giant, and now started to tell his tales....
«In the beginning of time, three Aesir gods traveled the young Earth
They were Odin, Loki and Hœnir
They travelled across mountains and un-built forests, and there was little nourishment...
In a valley, they came across a flock of oxen, and butchered one in the seydi, but the meat would not cook...
«I am the one who stops the meat from cooking!»
The eagle who spoke was not tiny
«If you will give me my share of the Sacred Meal, it will soon cook.»
The Aesir agreed to this...

As it turned out, the share of the giant in eagle's hide was the whole sacrifice...

Loki, that Deep-of-Soul Hiding Beast, who had been blowing at the fire for ages, became very angry...

Furious, the Friend of the Raven-God ran after the Sacrifice
And soon enough, Loki, whom all the gods perceive in chains, was stuck to the Ghost of the Giant World, that Wind-Flapping Vulture and Corpse-Thrower...
Please!!! I will do ANYTHING if you will just let me down!
«Never shall you be free from MY grasp, Child of Leaf Island...
... unless you swear to lead the Maiden Who Knows the Age-Cure of the Gods, Idunn, out of Ásgard!

Whatever else happened on this voyage is not told, but when The One Who Stirs the Stories got home, he went straight to the Goddess of the Well-Spring-Benches...
Do you know, Idunn, in a forest outside of Ásgard I saw some apples I think you would like....
«Bring your own apples, so you can compare them...»

And then, the Ale-Provider, that Eloquent, Knowledge-Hungy, Wonderful Maiden who Increases Divine Joy, was taken away by the Wing-Flapping King-Tricker...

And as soon as the Very Wise Father of the Giantess had taken The Seed of Yggdrasill out of the world of the Song-Smiths, the Wolf's Father, who had tried to save his life this way, realized that he was ageing, and rapidly....

All the Aesir gods soon began to age, and realized that their Drink-Serving Willow, she who was the Lover of All the Gods, that Knowledge-Hungry Goddess, the Youngest of the In-Ruler's Elders, was missing from the world of the gods....

They convened for a parliament by the Well of Origin, and it was soon enough revealed that Loki was the last to have been seen with the Maiden who is the Carrier of the Resounding Sun....

«If Freyia will lend me her falcon-hide, I shall soon return with the Grieving Woman,» Loki swore, promising to make right his wrong.
For this purpopse, Freyia gladly lent out her death-hide to him, and he flew into the giant world of the Drumming

When Loki arrived in the World of the Drumming, the Corpse-Fisher was out at sea...
But the Goddess of the Benches of the Returning Springs was at home... now donned in wolf-hide
He turned the Mead-Serving Maiden into a nut so that he could carry her out of that deadly realm...
But the Slave-Binding Corpse-Swallower, that treason-wise Mountain Howler, flew after the hawk, and his wings flapped so hard that Loki could hear the winds he made...

The Aesir saw Loki in Freyia's Death Hide approach rapidly, as if from out of the eyes of the pursuing and corpse-hungry eagle, and prepared a huge pyre by their wall...
The Wind-Diminishing Falcon flew through the fire with the Seed of Yggdrasill
But the Eagle caught fire....
That killing is widely known...
But the Eagle had fostered a maiden, Skadi, the goddess of skiing, she who hunted with bow and arrow in the windy and rocky mountains....
Skadi, who thrives among wolves.
Skadi, from Iron Forest.
Skadi, who demands Justice.
Skadi, who ensures Atonement.
Skadi, whose name is Injury

Skadi was offered a husband among the Aesir, one of her own choice. But she could not see his face when she chose, only the feet of the candidates.

She chose the most beautiful feet, for she believed they must belong to Balder from Broad Vision, on whom nothing is un-lovely.

But it turned out to be Njörd from Ships' Harbor, the ruler of winds and waves. He stood with his feet in the water every day, and thus had the prettiest pair.

Skadi accepted him for her husband.

In her terms for a truce, Skadi also demanded that the Aesir had to be able to make her laugh – a task that the Grim Bride of the Rocks and Mounds was absolutely certain that they would not ever manage!

But Loki knew exactly how to solve this near-doomed, impossible task...

BÆÆÆÆÆÆ!!!
VÆÆÆÆÆ!!!
Running about like a fool and hurt in his private parts, the Stirrer of the Stories fell right into the lap of Injury.
Then laughed Skadi...

Skadi brought her new husband back to her World of Drumming, but after nine nights, Njördr was unhappy....

Sad seemed to me, the mountains.
I stayed but nine nights there.
The howling of wolves seemed grim to me, compared to the song of swans.

Then the couple tried to live with Njörd at the Ships' Harbor.
But after nine nights, Skadi was unhappy...

I could not sleep in a bed by the sea, for the nasty schreeching from birds

He wakes me on his flight from the ocean, the seagull, every morning!

Then they got a divorce, and Skadi returned to rule the realm she inherited from her father.

But it is said that she later had many children by Odin, and from them, the royal dynasty of northern Norway descended...

Skadi has also been called the Goddess of Skiing, for she fares a-skiing and a-hunting in the wolf-ridden mountains
Then said Aegir, the Ocean Lord:
And Bragi, the skáld, replied:
This Slave-Binder — he cannot possibly have been an ordinary fellow! Do you know anything of his lineage?
The All-Powerful was his father…

«When his three sons were to share his legacy, they took an equal amount of gold into their mouths. This is why «gold» is hidden away in runes and poetry, so that we refer to it as «The Speech of the Giants»

ABOUT THE AUTHOR

Maria Kvilhaug was born in Oslo, Norway, in 1975. She studied History of Religions and Old Norse Philology at the university of Oslo. She has written several non-fiction and fiction books concerning Old Norse Pre-Christian culture and religion.

http://www.bladehoner.wordpress.com
http://www.youtubecom/user/ladyoft-helabyrinth

NON-FICTION:
The Maiden with the Mead (2004/2009)
The Seed of Yggdrasill (2013/2018/2020)
The Poetic Edda, Six Cosmology Poem (2017/2021)
The Trickster and the Thunder god, Thor and Loki in Old Norse Myths (2018)

FICTION:
Blade Honer Series:
The Hammer of Greatness
My Enemy´s Head
The He Rune´s Claim
A Twisted Mirror

The Three Little Sisters

The Three Little Sisters is an indie publisher that puts authors first. We specalize in the strange and unusual. From titles about pagan and heathen spirituality to traditional fiction we bring books to life.

https://the3littlesisters.com